Memoirs of a Street Urchin

by Louie Stride

Michael Luckly

A day in Bath,

Midsummer. 1985

'My head was close cropped like a boys because of lice, most children had them then!'

Edited by Graham Davis

ISBN 0 86197 051 9

Published by Bath University Press
The University of Bath
Claverton Down, Bath, England

Set in Garamond at the University of Bath
Printed by Dawson and Goodall Limited

Preface

In June 1983, I had just given a lecture during the Bath Festival entitled 'Unwelcome Visitors to Bath', when I was approached by Dr Marianna Clark of the Camden Works Museum about a manuscript written by a former tea-lady at the museum. Would I be interested to read it, and to interview the lady? From the brief details given of the material, I felt at once that this was going to be something quite out of the ordinary. So it proved to be.

The manuscript was written, partly in biro, partly in pencil, in an old, coverless exercise book. It has a scrap of paper cellotaped to the front page, and on it was written, 'I swear this is the truth understated', a phrase reminiscent of Victorian pamphlets on social reform. In some sixty pages of writing, dealing with the years 1907–1920, there was scarcely a single spelling mistake, but also few commas, and no paragraphs at all.

It came to be written in 1972, when Mrs Ross returned from Ireland to her native Bath, after an absence of six years. After an appalling childhood in the slums of Edwardian Bath, Mrs Ross had acquired a small cottage overlooking the open country towards Englishcombe village. Whilst living there, she had enjoyed the picking of wild flowers and hearing the sound of nightingales in Padleigh woods. The cottage was taken away from her by compulsory purchase and then demolished. On returning to Bath, Mrs Ross found that the site of her old cottage was built on with new bungalows. The bungalows were an affront to her sense of justice, and she was angry and bitter. All the suffering and hardship endured in Bath all those years ago seemed compounded by this final act of insensitive treatment. And it was this incident that prompted Louie Ross to set down the extraordinary experiences of her early life.

The curator of the Camden Works Museum, Frankie Repper, took an interest in the manuscript, and other loose sheets of writing, completed at various times, emerged to give details of Louie's working career. The museum kindly allowed me to see all the writing, some of which overlapped, and I was asked to consider its suitability for publication. Voraciously, I read everything in its various forms, and it all confirmed my first instinct about the work. My own view was that it required sympathetic editing with the intention of leaving it as unspoilt as possible, adding or amending here and there, only to make the meaning clear. Subsequently, in discussion with Dr Angus Buchanan and John Lamble at Bath University, I received support and encouragement for this approach. I typed out a version of the original, and Louie and I worked on the typescript together. In the process, other details kept emerging and a few points could be checked, as the text triggered off more memories. These were then incorporated where they belonged in her story.

The edited text differs only from the original in two minor changes. There are one or two things deleted, and the editor's insertions are included within square brackets. Responsibility for the layout and design of the text in chapters is mine. The writing itself contains the original colloquial expressions, truly representing the language Louie speaks, an unusual combination of street slang, interspersed with literary references and lines of poetry. Capital letters in mid-sentence are retained to preserve the intended emphasis, a practice incidentally found in the eighteenth century letters of the leisured classes.

Graham Davis

Introduction

Memoirs of a Street Urchin represents a remarkable example of working class autobiography. The story of Louie Stride, to use her maiden name, is extraordinary by any standards. Born, the illegitimate daughter of a prostitute mother, later to become the proud possessor of a drunken step-father, a childhood spent in virtual starvation, and moving from one slum district to another, it is an extreme case of social deprivation in a wealthy provincial city. But it is also a story of survival, that of a young girl living out of the gutter, stealing from shops, begging from neighbours, or taking advantage of the first tentative experiments of welfare provision. A wisdom and determination bred in the streets continued into the adult world of employment that was largely spent in hotel service. Here the product of the slums was to rub shoulders with gentility, and to record with wonder and a sense of irony what was served to guests already overweight, ostensibly visiting Bath for their health.

Most remarkably, the writing itself combines the influence of the slum environment, in the language of the streets, with a sense of the dramatic, in cameo descriptions of people and places, drawn from a childhood reading of Dickens and other popular writers. The writing engages the emotions, but also maintains a capacity to spring a surprise on the reader, as the following examples demonstrate:

'Just about this time, 1917, the powers that be recognised there was a problem with hunger amongst some families. . . . So a "canteen" came into being . . . in St. Michael's Place. . . . It was in the charge of an ex-navy man, I believe by name of Mark Lane, he did the cooking I do know. His wife was a very superior person, very much like Queen Alexandra, she wore high-necked blouses, and was a very austere person. Children from various schools were picked out for this special dinner every day, and I was . . . one of the lucky ones. Such food I can't describe, the smell alone would make me faint with delight at the anticipation of good things to come. One day, we would have lovely thick soup, and Mark Lane was seemingly severe, but one could see the pleasure behind the so masked face when he saw the gusto and enjoyment. We had second helpings, too, till everything was gone.'

Throughout the piece, food, or rather the lack of it, is a constant theme. The enormous pleasure expressed in the anti-cipation of some form of nourishment, a mug of hot milk, after fainting at school, a free dinner of thick soup, or a crust of bread found in the gutter, retain a marvellous sense of wonder. Yet it is as if hunger heightened the senses. The descriptions of people have a sharpness and astuteness that penetrates behind the public face.

Pathos and humour combine in this moving account of Louie returning home from a holiday in the country for deprived children, having been sent off with a paper parcel like one of the evacuees in the Second World War:

'So I went on the train with a lot of other kids, with our clothes in paper parcels. This was a different holiday, and I did not like it one bit. There were three of us billeted on an elderly couple, named Mr and Mrs Gale, and the village was called Gastard. Here we picked blackcurrants and did odd jobs, the like of which I'd never done, and didn't want to do. You see I was from a town, and there was always some diversion and people about. Here it was very lonely, and the couple were too old really. Also the two girls with me were sisters, and I was out of everything. I was glad when the three weeks was up, and I could go home. Most children had someone to meet them, not me! Oh no, Here I was again on the platform looking in vain for someone glad to see me. However, I met my stepfather on my way home, not quite blind drunk, as the saying goes, but nearly. I remember I burst into tears at the ignominy and injustice of it all, and then when I got home my mother was soaking her feet of all things, and not a sign of food. What a welcome, I remember thinking.'

At such times Louie could feel quite alone against the world. But although poor and uneducated and diminutive in stature, she was not lacking determination and spirit. In her life she had often fallen foul of authority, whether represented by the School Board Inspector, a health inspector, or an employer, but if the need arose, she could stick up for herself, as she did in front of an Employment Tribunal in the 1930s:

'One day, while at Weston-super-Mare, I had a notification to go to a Board Meeting of Officials re my Cards and week's wage, and lo and behold I had this most important document, to say it was a Travel Document to a Tribunal at Taunton, that my day's expenses would be paid, i.e. lunch and any wages lost. I felt dreadfully important I can tell you, and so I found this place at Taunton at the time appointed. And was I scared, I had to go before an awful lot of elderly gentlemen sitting around a large table, poor little me stood at one end, and had to answer questions. However, my courage returned although I was certainly very overawed by the occasion. So I stood up bravely and asked, (in reply to the question why had I left) "If any of you gentlemen present know what the inside of a large catering establishment was like?" I stated I had experience of Hotels for a few years, and in the one I was in a Kitchen Porter always did the work I was asked to do at the Cadena, and [I] was quite unfit to do it, and so I was given a week's wages, and the Cards had already been returned via the Labour Exchange.'

The personal dimension of this life story has its own intrinsic interest, but beyond that there is a genuine historical value in these brief memoirs. Louie Stride's story provides information and insights largely unknown or ignored previously. We learn of the existence of considerable numbers of street urchins, immortalised by Dickens in 'Oliver Twist' in early Victorian London, still present in Edwardian Bath. The account reveals the incidence of desertion and the hiding of soldiers during the First World War in slum districts devoid of men who had been conscripted into the forces. We are reminded of the casual nature of prostitution among poor women, a subject of much current scholarship, and of the wide social spectrum that served as clients. Valuable insights are provided in establishing that there was a hierarchy of slums within the city, something unrevealed by contemporary written accounts as I have argued in my doctoral thesis on Victorian Bath. In her experiences, we have to recognise the power of the moral stigma against illegitimacy that had become operative in working class districts everywhere except perhaps in the very worst places like the Dolemeads. Moreover, we see that in the first fitful experiments of welfare provision for the urban poor, connections with benefactors and not a little guile were necessary before obtaining relief.

This is history from below, the perspective of the labouring poor, in contrast with the traditional emphasis on the dates of Parliamentary legislation, and on the deeds of the famous and powerful members of society. Its importance lies in qualifying the traditional version of our national story. For instance, the Education Act of 1870, followed by a local borough bye-law in 1878, made elementary education compulsory in Bath. Louie, and the children she grew up with were blithely innocent of the majesty of Parliament, or of the writ of the Town Council and the School Board. To them, the School Board Inspector was a figure of ridicule. Her impression was that compulsory schooling was introduced in about 1916. Truancy remained a normal condition for at least a section of the urban poor for more than a generation after the Education Act of 1870.

Interestingly, too, in the light of so much recent historical study on the subject, we gain important insights into central features of urban working class culture. The spirit of opportunism that thrived on a knowledge of the streets and its people showing that personal contacts were essential for survival. A practical morality that was strong on neighbourliness, but in which there was no contest between thieving and starving. Above all, there was a pride and a toughness to withstand the relentless grind and the inevitable misfortunes inherent in a state of poverty.

Chapter 1

So I came in contact with my first hand-cart. This was one of the most useful articles of those times, everybody used them for all sorts of purposes, the main one being 'doing a Moonlight Flit'.

In the year 1907 when I was born there was not any Welfare State bounties, or societies for unmarried mothers etc, if one had been 'unfortunate' as did sometimes happen such as in my mothers case, one was often turned out of the family home owing to the disgrace and resultant gossip in poor neighbourhoods. In better off circumstances the offending daughter would be banished to another relative or some friend in another town or anywhere where one wasn't very well known. I was one such illegitimate child, my natural father was a Welshman from Merthyr Tydfil, he was to me a hateful man often came for the week-end and I did hate him, his name was Arthur Burton who knows maybe one of 'the' Burtons.

I was born in the Queen City of the west, but in a very peculiar place, namely the old Gaol in Grove Street, now a block of luxury flats, I believe. Of my mother's family I know very little, I saw one brother only once. My mother's family had been a respectable family but came down in the world, one of her forbears was a well known builder, he was known as 'Gracious Stride', he built the artisan houses in Broad Street Place and others in the Walcot area. The brothers names were Jack and Albert. The name is still on the opposite wall at Broad Street Place 'Gracious Court' engraved in the stone.

We were living in a little Court in a small terrace of cottages in Walcot Street by the side of the public house called the Hat and Feather which I believe is still in being but the cottage and all the artisan dwellings gone long since. The day I remember the soldier in the dazzling uniform seems like yesterday, my mother left me in his charge while she went out to work and I was at the crawling stage, but he had an assignment with his girl friend and while they were canoodling I disgraced myself and when my mother returned they had a row and I never saw him again! He was so splendid had very colourful uniform on of a Bandsman in the Somerset Light Infantry, gold braid and such bright brass buttons.

Not long after this incident we had to move. There could be two reasons, my mother maybe was turned out for non-payment of rent, but I expect the real reason was my presence and no husband visible, and such things were unheard of. So I came in contact with my first hand cart. This was one of the most useful articles of those times, everybody used them for all sorts of purposes, the main one being 'doing a Moonlight Flit'. This meant when one couldn't pay the rent which was very often in the poor areas, one hired a Handcart. The payment was 1/6 deposit and 6d per hour for the use of. One had to be quick, load up and away, mostly in the dead of night so as not to get caught by the landlord and to get the deposit back. I don't ever remember us moving at night but in the evening before too late.

Our first move was from this Hat and Feather court to Walcot House. This was a very nice period house which has since been demolished to make room for a block of flats.

My mother used to go to work cleaning shops, mostly in Northumberland Passage in the centre of Bath, and her wages were 6d an hour. She worked at several shops there and left me in the charge of a girl in the house. The first shop on the left was a milliners, 'Roadhouse' I think the name was, also she did for Pearces the paper shop, but the one I remember most was a Mr Potts the chemist in the corner at the back of Crooks gents hat shop. My mother treated Mr Potts very badly, she stole a lot of household linen, used to come home with sheets and pillow cases around her waist under her skirt. These articles we used to sit and patiently pick out the markings in the corners which were in red cotton. Then in various stages they would be taken to the pawnshop in the Upper Borough Walls, 'Lawson Howes' by name. It was of course never redeemed and what happened to the tickets I don't remember. Mr Potts was a rotund little gentleman and bald, very much like Mr Pickwick in one of my books.

Anyway whatever happened we did not stay long at the Walcot House, here we had the Handcart ride again, me perched on top of the furniture. I remember we had some quite nice pieces, to start with a mahogany Pembroke table and family photo album, but it all got less and less as my mother sold it off to pay rent. I do believe the furniture shop is still there where we used to sell it off bit by bit. We ended up with an orange box and our clothes and the barest of necessities.

This move now was a long way across the town with my mother pushing as best she could to a small hovel type of cottage up a steep hill called Holloway. It was at the back of a sweet shop called Cowleys. The man used to make all types of boiled sweets, lovely gob stoppers of all types and sizes, peppermint, cloves, and ginger. His shop window was a picture in colours and stripes. I think he supplied shops and had another one in Broad Street. We arrived at this place, who owned or how she got to hear of these different places I'll never know. All I can recollect is the next morning all the women in the surrounding cottages attacked my mother verbally and in person called her a 'Scarlet Woman', and they threw her goods out in the yard, 'coming to live in amongst a lot of decent

'This move now was a long way across the town with my mother pushing as best she could to a small hovel type of cottage up a steep hill called Holloway.'

people with a Bastard', they weren't going to tolerate that and they didn't.

It's hard to believe in this day and age that such a thing took place, but to me it was one of the most humiliating days of my life. How old would I be, I'd say 2½ to 3 if that, so we trudged off to find somewhere else with the goods on the cart and me on top as usual, we found a room back in the old Walcot area again not far from our first abode. It was known as Georges Buildings, and we had a downstairs room. Here I was weaned and went to my first school, yes I was on the breast till I was 3 years old and running about, and it was more or less my only means of sustenance, and I attribute my wiriness to this fact. It was a hard job to get me weaned, some folk told her to use this and some folk said that, bitter aloes and a black mask with holes in it did the trick eventually.

Here I was sent to Walcot Infants School and I remember the young teacher giving me a nice warm dress which my mother took to the pawnshop and I never saw it again. We stayed here for quite a while. I suppose the landlord had to evict eventually because my next ride was to a house in Ballance Street on the Julian Road, can't remember the number but about half way up.

Here I had a most memorable experience. It seems as time went on and my mother got more and more persecuted and couldn't get money, she turned to prostitution in a quiet sort of way. I might add too that she was odd, I noticed she was not like the other children's mothers and I was always dressed very peculiarly in old fashioned clothes. However while we were in Ballance Street she picked up with some man, I would know him now, and she took me to his house to sleep. I was instructed not to cough or make any noise, the house was in Portland Place, and I do know the name of the people but maybe best not to mention. Anyway I remember being in a lovely room in a [beautiful] four poster bed but I woke up in our quarter in Ballance Street! The next day there was an awful to do. When I came home from school and my mother from work (yes she still had her shop jobs in Northumberland Passage), the room had been ransacked, everything was upside down and such a muddle, whether it was the police or the owner of the house we'd slept in that had forced an entry I know not. Only that it seems something valuable was missing and she had stolen it. So of course the usual thing happened, we had notice to quit.

One thing I have omitted to say is the continual hunger we endured. Rent used to be 1/6 to 2/6 a week and the few shillings my mother earned charring did not give adequate sustenance,

'All I can recollect is the next morning all the women in the surrounding cottages attacked my mother verbally and in person called her a 'scarlet woman', and they threw her goods out in the yard. . . .'

8

'Here I was sent to Walcot Infants School and I remember the young teacher giving me a nice warm dress which my mother took to the pawn-shop and I never saw it again.' (Louie Stride is sitting on the teacher's right)

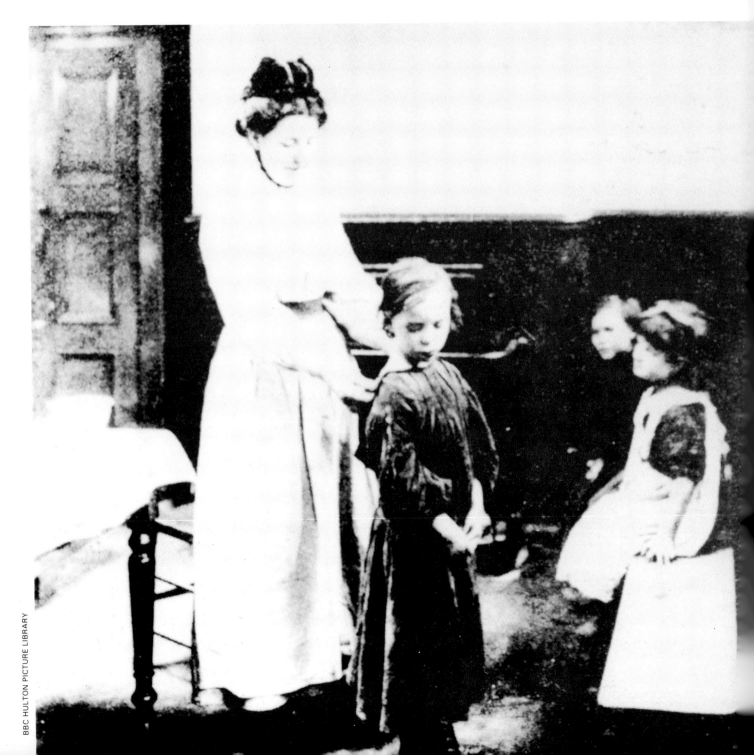

'If one had lice, one was given a pink card with instructions to give to your parents and how to get rid of them. I always had one but used to tear it up and put it down the grating somewhere on the way home.'

just sporadic meals of bread and tea, so I was in a perpetual state of hunger and would do anything for food. At the school I would steal from younger children, can you picture it me 4 years old or so, grabbing an infants piece of bread and running into a lavatory to eat it. Of course I was pounced upon by the older brothers and sisters, and called names and treated badly as only children can. They can be very cruel. I was known as Lulu 'nodrawers', which I suppose was a fact. How I hated that school! The headmistress was a Miss Smith and could be like everybody else nasty. There was however one young teacher there, Miss Padfield, I think it was her who gave me the dress. She took me once to a little cafe that used to be at the Walcot Boys entrance. It was run by a man called Imber, and he used to specialise in Rice pudding, this pudding had a lovely brown skin on top and used to be sold at ½d a slice. He used to be sick of our hungry faces looking at him through the window I know. This teacher, Miss Padfield I believe her name was, took me up once for a glass of hot milk and I well remember how lovely it was. [I] can never taste or smell hot milk to this day without recalling that bitter cold Monday morning when she was so kind, but I believe she was reprimanded by the head and didn't do it again.

My head was close cropped like a boys because of lice, most children had them then! Also very early in the morning if we had 3d, I would have to be up six or sevenish to go to the Bakeries for stale bread. There would be an army of kids all ages and sizes and we would wait patiently in the rain and cold, the winters then seemed very cold! The first stop would be Red House in Walcot Street, if no stale bread there we would all rush down to Fortts in Green Street, and if none there we would have to go down to the main Bakery in Manvers Street, such a long way for little tired legs and hungry bellies. The men who opened up were most kind. If [there was] plenty of stale bread about one would get a nice pillow case full for 3d, we always took pillow cases. Sometimes one of them would put in a surreptitious bun and give you a wink, my how we would

feast going home! [There were] no school dinners in those days and that's when they were needed.

Chapter 2

And so I grew up scavenging food where I could, in the gutter pretty often, surprising what one could find edible. I ran wild during the day, and was locked in at night.

Our next move was to 22A Broad Street, a top big attic over the present Health Food shop. This house was let out to several people, unfurnished rooms, and very nice it was. We had a nice view of the street and from here I could see such a lot. I well remember the Bath Race days, the horses were led on foot and the ostlers and jockeys and all the horse brakes and carts taking people up Lansdown. Here I was shut in a lot while my mother was out working and doing her other nefarious business. I knew what she was up to and accepted her way of life, could do no other could I?

I was a very lonely child, and a veritable Ishmael. No-one wanted to make friends with me, dirty and ragged as I was more or less. At this address we at last seemed settled, and it was simply wonderful, (I was 5 years old by now) for why? Well the agent of the owner of the house, instead of having the rent, he had goods in kind! So this was my last ride on the handcart and we were at last secure. In the room underneath us was a very nice old lady, at least she seemed old to me. Her name was Mrs Orchard, not quite sure, but she used to give me a dinner very often when my mother was out, and I was forbidden to go out. Sometimes I did not see my mother all day. I would go to school down the long steps on the Paragon and back again, no food mark you very often, and if I could I would pick up a cat to keep me company. Anybody's cat would do, but I am very previous. The widow Mrs Archard left, she could not stand how things were going, in fact all the tenants left, and we had the place to ourselves. This suited the agent as he could visit us at any time and that was that! So at night when it was dark and I was frightened, I would have this cat to nurse and cuddle, and I do believe cats saved my sanity because like all children of 5 years or so I was scared of the dark, curly stairs, but a pussy to talk to was something tangible. Of course they all fled as soon as my mother used to come home but I would get another. I dread to think what the house must have smelt like.

I did miss the widow lady and her dinners, it was the only dinners I ever saw on a plate! We subsisted on a bit of boiled rice and bread if lucky. Sometimes when we were in the money, i.e. 6d, I would be sent down to 'Old Charlies' in Walcot Street. He had a little huxters shop come cafe. I think he did all the ostlers meals at the Saracens Head, and the draymen, also the farmers and men who worked at the Cattle Market just opposite on market days. Here I would get a 'top' of a loaf, used to be called cottage loaves, had a small top on a flat bottom and a hole down the centre. I would get a top for 2d, ½d of skimmed milk, ½d worth of tea, 1d of sugar, ½d worth of St Ivels cheese (this was like a cottage cheese, I would get a small screw in a bag like a funnel), ½d worth of firewood, or if winter, no cheese, or a 1d briquet, this was a square lump of solidified coal dust enough to make a fire. Just imagine 2½ new pence! Ah well, it taught me the value of money and how to shop if nothing else.

There was another shop in Broad Street which I loved to go into for tea. It was called the 'Old Cha Ya', and kept by a very tall aesthetic looking gentleman. I'm sure he used to dread me coming into his high class shop. My order would be, 'halfpenny worth of tea dust please', from the tea chests! He always treated me with the utmost kindness and I felt very grown up in his presence, why I don't know, but I must have been very precocious having to fend for myself, and I daresay I was cheeky too.

So we went on, sometimes I went to school and sometimes I didn't, perhaps I had no footwear or most likely was ill for want of food and I stayed home. Schooling in those days was not really compulsory, but laws were beginning to be made to alter this, and a School Board Inspector was introduced, and his job would be to look for all the truants in the different areas. I believe he covered the whole Bath area, anyway many's the time he would peep through the glass door at the bottom of the stairs and say, 'I can see you', and I used to fly upstairs and keep quiet. His name was Mr Billet, and he lived opposite what was then the workhouse. All us kids played him up in lots of different ways, and I was very sorry later in life when I saw his mentally handicapped son and all he had to contend with, but he was a real thorn in the flesh to me during childhood and I disliked him.

At this school was a 'humped back', now known as Spina Bifida, she was my age and known as Hump Back Annie. She had a lovely face and taught me a very valuable lesson which I've never forgotten, and that was to count my blessings. I used to look at her and say to myself, 'Well, I'm pretty ugly looking but I've got my right shape and faculties', young, hungry, and lonely as I was, I realised it could be worse.

I've often wondered why there was no public body to do something in such cases as mine was, it just seemed as if all turned a blind eye. I remember near one Christmas a lady stopping us in the street and giving me a small gift of a Christmas stocking, a little net one with several sweets and little toys in it. I was overjoyed and kept that for years as one of my precious gifts. Can't quite recall her name, Miss Lindsay was it, but could take you to her house at Beechen Cliff on the Bear Flat. She was some type of unofficial social worker I guess. We went to her house 'begging', I remember the maid turned us away.

And so I grew up scavenging food where I could, in the gutter pretty often, surprising what one can find edible. I ran wild during the day, and was locked in at night. The Agent (won't mention names as the family is a well known Bath one at the present day) called regularly for his 'dues', which were paid in kind but not in money, and I was sent on an errand on these occasions. Also my father from Wales called occasional weekends. I suppose he was a married man, anyway call he did, and I loathed him. I was also thoroughly ashamed at the way he dressed. He was a 'navvy' of some kind I should imagine as he wore 'Yorks', i.e. straps beneath the knees and a type of leather trousers which were worn by outdoor and heavy workers of the times 1912 or so.

And so we stayed at 22A Broad Street and no more handcart rides for which I was thankful. About this time I learned to read. I started school at 3 years of age but was pretty dim, I think, as I was always being chastised because other children would read and I couldn't, and then all at once I could, it was marvellous. My mother still did her charring jobs at Northumberland Passage and brought me picture books, fairy stories and all sorts of books. She was a great book collector herself, but I don't think she read very much. Instead of the money for her work, she had books, and many's the day I expected food but none was forthcoming, and she bought books, and I also fear she stole as well.

I read books much too advanced or old for me, but recall them well, and the pleasure they gave, and made me forget my awful loneliness. I read J. M. Barrie and Gene Stratton Porter,

'*Our next move was to 22A Broad Street, a top big attic over the present Health Food shop. . . . Here I was shut in a lot while my mother was out working and doing her other nefarious business.*'

how I loved the 'Girl of the Limberlost' and 'The Cardinal', and later in life, 'The Keeper of the Bees'. I went through a lot of Dickens too, my two favourites being, 'The Christmas Carol' (which I still have the actual one), and 'The Old Curiosity Shop'. I told myself Little Nell was better off than I was, all I had was a mad mother! I also made the acquaintance of a writer who gave me much pleasure named Louis Wain. He wrote only about cats and stories of cats. He went mad, I believe, the more insane he became the more delightful the cats became. But my favourites were the ones about food such as in the Brothers Grimm, where children would be hungry, and a fairy would given them a magic wand and say, 'Table be covered!' How my mouth used to water, and I would conjure up the food I would choose!

I still took in any cat for company in the evenings when she locked me in and went 'out on the streets', as she called her, what would be called 'moonlighting' now, i.e. spare job. Sometimes, she came home with 1/6, that was the 'fee', and mostly without anything to eat. I was a marvel to survive the malnutrition as I did, and I put the fact to being breast fed, it must have been a good foundation, although I was very small and diminutive.

Chapter 3

Just fancy that, for me a Dad at last! Now nobody could scoff and sneer at me any more. Of course me being nine years old didn't know as much as I thought I did!

So the 1914 War loomed nearer, and I was 7 years, 2 months when it was declared. I remember the day so well, and all the regulations it brought with it. The troops started being recruited, and bands marching, and the songs that were sung. I knew them all, Blighty, and Tipperary, and Keep the Home Fires Burning. I had a very retentive memory and could sing them all. I daresay my bit of Welsh ancestry made me a music lover too. All the songs of earlier years I could sing to myself, the ones my mother sang to keep me quiet, 'Who were you with last night?', and 'I wouldn't leave my little wooden hut for you', and 'Bill Bailey won't you come home', and poems too.

So it went on till 1915, we were living a bit better now, not quite such hunger. My mother got very bold and brought men back to the attic, and I would discreetly disappear. It would be soldiers, and of course no shortage of them as Bath had a lot of big houses and schools that were taken over as billets. In 1916, there was a contingent of Canadian soldiers who came to Prior Park College, and one of these called regularly. In fact, he was there so much that the others kept away. He had some reason to want to stay in England, and to my great joy, they were married. Just fancy that, for me a Dad at last! Now nobody could scoff and sneer at me any more. Of course me being nine years old didn't know as much as I thought I did!

However, it meant my mother would not go out 'on the streets' any more, and she didn't either, also it meant food, and that was my main gain. But alas, I also didn't know he was a hopeless alcoholic. One was used so much to drunkenness in the poor it didn't get noticed. He was a slightly wounded soldier, in the knee, nothing much, he was pulling a fast one to get out of the war and all its carnage. He was in the Royal Highlanders of Canada, and was quite a good looking man especially in uniform. He was a good deal older than my mother. The Canadians were paid a lot more than the British Tommies, and it used to cause friction I well remember. What did I care if he was drunk? I used to wait down the street and hold his hand all the way home. I was so proud my mum was married, and believe me I told the world, no hiding away for me any more I was as good as the rest.

Whether they went off and got married in a drunken bout, and he didn't know what he was doing I just can't think, but the fact remained, and I think he did regret it. My mother, as I said earlier on was odd. Whether it was the fact of having me and being turned out, which was a heinous sin in those days, or the resultant starvation, or maybe the drugs she was using not to contract venereal disease, I just don't know but her mental condition certainly was deteriorating. He didn't seem to notice, and me? Well she was always queer and that was it. It was only in a quiet way, she would sit by herself for hours on end and talk to herself very quietly and she would crochet lace and knit. She was very industrious in this way, but at the last corner of the lace tablecloth, or whatever, she would go awry. Poor soul, who knows what torments of conscience she suffered? She died many years after in an asylum.

However, here I was in proud possession of a man in my life for the first time really belonging. I made all sorts of plans in my mind, and the first one would be to get away from that awful Walcot School. His plan was to get demobbed, as they called it, and he would get a good gratuity, and this is what happened. It took a good while though as the war was going badly then in 1916, and he was only slightly wounded. He got demobbed, but he did not get the money like he expected. It used to come by cheque in smallish amounts, and then he would have plenty of food, and he would have plenty of booze.

He was, however, a kindly man to me, and I was never afraid of him as I was of most men. He told me all about Canada, how he stowed away in the ship Montrose, the one Crippen was on, and worked for the Canadian Pacific Railway as a back woodsman. They started at a place called Fields, I think, and how the huge trees were felled and sent down the rivers. Also how they had to keep watch by the camp fires all night because of animals, bears mostly, and how when they had to leave they went to Vancouver and spent their money. He told me of the cold of Ontario, how the cutlery would be frozen to the tables in the morning, and told me of Kicking Horse Canyon, and the Great Divide and Niagara Falls, and all sorts of wonderful things, and I was interested in it all. Sounded worth seeing, and I made a resolve there and then I would go to see all those wonderful things, but did I? No, I'm very sorry to say. Life goes so quickly, and we mean to do so much!

Until his demob he had to live at Prior Park where he was stationed, and from there he could bring food, cheese and such like things, at least we were never so hungry as in former times. But came a rude awakening, didn't the Agent find out about the wedding, and we had to go at once, such a scene. I don't know whether he thought she was a permanent mistress or whatever, but I do know we never had any money or food from him just the free attic for services rendered. Anyway, my step father had to move fast to get us out and our belongings. He got a most

'It was a one up and one down cottage, a misnomer owned by Bowlers, aerated water company and plumbers, in a small backyard in behind a row of houses in Great Corn Street.'

dreadful place, all he could find in a hurry, and cheap it had to be as he had not received the gratuity, only bits and pieces at a time, and that was soon disposed of in the pubs on himself, my mother never drank intoxicants at any time.

It was a one up and one down cottage, a misnomer, owned by Bowlers, aerated water company and plumbers, in a small back yard in behind a row of houses in Great Corn Street. It must have been there before the terrace of houses was built, they were large houses and I daresay at one time good class people dwelt there, and maybe this hovel, for that was all it was, belonged to the stables or some such thing. It was so dark after our lovely attic, tap in the yard, but no other facilities that I can recall, we must have used a bucket! We moved in, but the next thing I knew my step father had joined up with the British Expeditionary Forces. What made him do this? It must have been the fact that he couldn't get a job, or rather he did get one but it was street sweeping and he was bit above that. Suffice to say he joined up and we were back to square one as they say. One thing he didn't do a bunk as he could have done, we wouldn't have been any the wiser, but we thought he had as the Army allowance was such a long time coming.

I used to sit out on the pavement obeying my mother's instruction to wait for the postman. Of course, I was not going to school, in fact I did very little schooling the whole of my school life, between having no boots to wear, I wore hob nails a size too small always as they were a shilling cheaper or else no food, and I suffered so frequently from fainting and nervous collapse that I just was not able. But the new Education Act was in force and in consequence my mother was summoned for my non-attendance on two occasions. The first was a caution, and the next time a fine of five or ten shillings luckily after the soldiers allowance came through. The forms had not been completed correctly, hence the long hold up. We did get the back money and such feeds we had then.

Another thing was my name Stride, I just did not like being known by it, and thereby letting everyone know I was a Bastard child. So seeing as now my mother was Mrs Jack Smith (wasn't his real name but he was known by it in Canada) so I'd listened to many of his tales of his former life before he went to Canada. He was from Birmingham and undoubtedly the black sheep of the family, at least that's what he told. I had the vaguest idea what this meant but took it all in, even to his home address. Oh yes, I had a very retentive memory alright and a highly vivid imagination, fantasy was my lifeline. There was several schools in this area, this part of Bath was the opposite end entirely to where we lived formerly. My plan was (I did just what I liked!) to go to a new school (I had one in mind having sounded out several kids and having looked round), I would go under my new name and also say I'd come from Birmingham, and give that address. This, believe it or not, is what I did.

It was a lovely school, girls only, called Kingsmead Board School, why 'board' I never found out. I used to look for 'boards' but couldn't find 'em! The Infant School was mixed but at seven years old the boys went to Bathforum, which was on a corner of Monmouth Street. The Headmaster was a kindly gentleman, named Mr Prosser, to me he seemed very aged, but I don't suppose he was. He used to call on the governess at times but there was no contact between the schools otherwise. The governess took to me immediately and I was accepted. I expect I was a sketch, nine years old and doing my own thing with a vengeance. I was tested and put in a class, of course all the lessons were completely strange, such things as grammar and queer types of arithmetic I'd never heard of. However, I liked it, got on seemingly alright, under my new name, and I was on top of the world. Then one day who should walk into the school classroom but my old enemy, Mr Billett the school board man? To say I nearly dropped dead with fright was putting it mildly. I'd quite forgotten about him, and of course being new to the school, I was in the front row. Well I'd been humiliated enough before but it was nothing to my present situation. He hauled me out in front of everybody and said why had I told such lies about my name and saying I'd come from Birmingham. I was in a state and I never lived it down. The governess was an understanding woman, and I daresay realised why I'd done it. She had all types in her life and was an ideal person for the job, some difference to my previous experience.

The army papers came eventually, but we were very short of food, and the rent was two and sixpence a week. The house in part, and the one next door was owned by a family named Bowler. One part was a ginger beer factory. [It was] put in funny bottles with a marble at the top, I never figured out how they were put in. Another part was an ironmongery department. One of the Bowler brothers did one business, selling nuts and bolts and all sorts of tools and the other did the ginger beer. I never did taste any, and the crates used to be stacked along the pavement both empty and full ones. I don't believe any were ever stolen either. In the Bowler family, there were two sisters, one a 'Head' nurse, she used to go round the schools and inspect the heads. If one had lice, one was given a pink card with instructions to give to your parents and how to get rid of

17

them. I always had one but used to tear it up and put it down the grating somwhere on the way home. I did clean myself of the vermin when I was about twelve with something called Sassafras Oil. It is a very effective cure but such a potent smell, stink the classroom out and the hair all oil. My hair was always shorn so it didn't matter. The other Bowler sister was something or other in the Clinic, situated in the Georgian houses in Kingsmead Square, but I was quite beneath her notice. I could never understand why they were so unkind, never to give me a bite of food, seeing as how they lived next door and saw me sitting in all weathers on the pavement outside.

The woman who lived in the house in front of us, number fourteen, was a big, fat, motherly woman, named Mrs Perrett. She had six children, one was a cripple, a boy younger than myself. My mother always kept to herself, and if anything was required, it was my job to do her bidding. She wasn't cruel or unkind in any way except for ignoring my presence more or less. Her attitude had always been that as I wasn't supposed to be there, I wasn't, and I was ignored accordingly, but she could be very violent if aroused, and she always threatened me that she would send me to the nuns if I ever told anyone I was hungry. This was because once when I was much younger and we passed a cake shop in Cheap Street, Shapleys, (afterwards Marks and Werry's), and I yelled my head off. I wanted one of the buns in the window, and a passer-by fetched a policeman, and I never asked or let anyone know by word or deed ever again that I was hungry. The threat of the orphanage and the nuns hung over me like the proverbial sword of Damocles.

What I did not know was how much better off I would have been, so life went on. I was very dirty and lousy, and when I used to appear at this neighbours door, she used to shoo me away. My mother had a bad habit of sending me to borrow a sixpence, and I don't think she was a good repayer of debts, and of course this woman had six children of her own, and her army allowance didn't allow for any spares. We had really quite a good allowance, it was a 'ring' paper affair not unlike the motor log book of today. We had the princely sum of nineteen and sixpence a week, that was fifteen shillings for the wife and four and sixpence for me, but she was a bad manager and we had food for the first two or three days of the week and then misery. I got into the habit of stealing from her purse, perhaps sixpence or a shilling, and then waiting till the end of the week when we had nothing, and coming home with some bread, and saying I'd picked up sixpence. But it didn't always work, I think she got wise to it.

Owing to the fact that she was summoned for my non-attendance at school, no matter how ill I was I had to go now, and she would take me by the hand and leave me in, mostly on Monday mornings, as I would be so weak for want of food. As long as I showed up and got my register mark I used to feel 'safe', at least she wouldn't be summoned again, and so on Mondays I answered the register and promptly fainted. This happened several Mondays, and I supposed it was noticed amongst the teachers and this wise old governess. And when it happened the third or fourth time I was carried out to the window on the stairs and given water as usual, but this time one of the teachers spoke up and said, 'Perhaps Louie would like a bun from next door?' (there was a Chinese restaurant next door). Well, my face must have lit up at the thought of it. The teachers were around me in a group, I remember, and one went for a bun and some milk. Well, the way I grabbed the bun and wolfed it told them all. I can remember one young one being in tears, Miss Woodward was her name. The others were Miss Burchel, Miss Jobbins, and Miss Roach, the Headmistress. Suffice to say I didn't faint on Monday or any other day any more. They clubbed around and sent me out for hot milk and virol every day, and also paid for me to have a dinner in a cafe in Abbey Green. The governess knew I would be in trouble with my mother over this, and she used to tell me to go ten minutes or so earlier than usual. This was marvellous Monday till Friday, how I fared week-ends I quite forget, but I suppose I was sustained better and no more fainting.

'Then one day who should walk into the school classroom but my old enemy, Mr Billett the school board man. . . . He hauled me out in front of everybody and said why had I told such lies about my name and saying I'd come from Birmingham.'

Chapter 4

So I would sit on the cold pavements with a pin and pick out these snails. It would be good protein I daresay! Had the best myself and took some into my mother, but not everything, she would be too suspicious as to how I came by it.

To go back to this working class district, and it was 'working' in every sense of the word, there was no dole or poor relief, or at least only in exceptional cases, i.e. cripples or bad illness, and even then people were too proud to let anyone know and then the relieving officer, as they were known, would come nosing round, so it was seldom anyone didn't work. This part of the city was a real hive of industry and commerce on a small scale. There were innumerable 'Totters', i.e. rag and bone men. Bath was always an affluent city, and the neighbourhoods where the 'nobs' lived was a regular round for these folks. Some had the proverbial handcarts, some prams, and some only on their backs in sacks, and one in particular very affluent one, he was known as 'Donkey Ball', sold wood chumps and had a donkey and cart, and his wife always went with him on his rounds. Others sold goods on the pavements outside their houses, old clothes, pots and pans, any and everything. Many had little shops, two in particular I remember, one was a lovely lady, Aunty Clare, who made and cooked faggots and peas. If only one could get hold of sixpence, or even threepence, and took a basin, she would be most generous, and the smell of those fragrant faggots are with me to this day. Another man [had] a baker and huxter shop, sold everything, not allowed now, parrafin and candles, and salt fish, and everything one could imagine. His name was a Mr Ollis, very clean and tidy he was. He also went out with a basket selling cooked snails and winkles, and I used to waylay him with a cup and if he had any over I would beg for some and I was never refused. Two other shops were in great demand that sold everything was Mrs Shortman and Mr Rowe around the corner. He was very good value for broken biscuits.

[The streets were full of 'characters' who somehow made a living]. One I remember was 'Badger' Pope, a very strong man who used to do outrageous things to attract attention, such as biting the heads off rats, or encouraging people to hit a concrete slab on his chest with a sledgehammer. I don't think anybody ever gave him any money. Then there were others like Guinea Pig Jack in the Corridor, and Blind Alice in the Ambury, and a blind man called Webb, with a tin cup, who was led around by one of his children.

So I would sit on the cold pavement with a pin and pick out these snails. It would be good protein I daresay! Had the best myself and took some into my mother, but not everything, she would be too suspicious as to how I came by it. There were dozens and dozens of children like myself, deprived and certainly had the making of juvenile delinquents, but I don't think many of us did. We all stole, yes, but only for our immediate needs. On our way to school was a fish and fruiterers, it was run by a man named Harry Wetten, and I'm quite sure he used to shut his eyes to an awful lot. The veg and fruit would be outside and as we went by we would surreptitiously steal, or rather 'whip' a carrot or anything, even a cabbage leaf, and I remember one time I got away with a kipper. I ate it raw, as it was in the playground and stunk the classroom out! Nobody bothered, they thought I was lucky!

Just about this time, 1917, the powers that be recognised there was a problem with hunger amongst some families, and decided to do something about it. So a 'canteen' came into being. It was in St Michaels Place, or St Michaels something, and I believe it is now a meals on wheels centre. It was in the charge of an ex-navy man, I believe by name of Mark Lane, he did the cooking I do know. His wife was a very superior person, very much like Queen Alexandra, she wore high necked blouses and was a very austere person. Children from various schools were picked out for this special dinner every day, and I was (thanks to that governess Miss Roach), one of the lucky ones. Such food I can't describe, the smell alone would make me faint with delight at the anticipation of good things to come. One day, we would have lovely thick soup, and Mark Lane was seemingly severe, but one could see the pleasure behind the so masked face when he saw the gusto and enjoyment. We had second helpings, too, till everything was gone. Then another day it would be steamed, spotted dick, a

GUINEA PIG-JACK OF BATH

pudding cooked in a cloth, and unmasked at the end of the table, and gee whiz that nectar and ambrosia and a bit of sugar was something to be talked about all the afternoon. There were three from our school! Perhaps I hadn't better mention names. Then another day would be rice on a plate, another day rice pudding, one didn't have the two, it was war time remember, and things were going pretty badly. Another day would be bread and cheese, and cocoa usually on a Friday, as this did not entail much washing up. The cheese was hard old stuff put through a mincer, and we had it in 'nobs' on the bread, and squashed down into it with our fingers. Famine did you say? It sure was, but not so bad as of yore for me, and I was well! Really nothing much the matter with me what a good meal couldn't cure.

My chief occupation when out of school was sitting on the curbstone watching all the world go by. There was a place of worship of some sort on the opposite side of the street called an Episcopal chapel, at least that was written over the door in large letters. I could never figure out what it meant, and don't know even now, all I noticed a lot of elderly ladies used to frequent there various evenings of the week. My games and playing consisted of a game called Five Stones, you had five little pebbles, and one tossed them, and if they all fell on the back of your hand at once, you had won, no winnings, just the skill counted.

The house on the other side of us, or our passage way rather, housed a very nice quiet family named Cottle, papersellers they were, and on the other side of them a very large family, and boisterous with it, especially weekends when both Pa and Ma would be inebriated. He was a Dustman, known today as a Refuse Collector. On the next side of this family dwelt a Coal Merchant, real posh they were, named Spurrell, and in spite of the father and sons being coal black, they had a nice house. None of the children were ever nasty to me, not like the Walcot horrors, I was just ignored mostly, some would be generous and lend me a go with their Whip and Top, or perhaps let me

21

have a run with their Hoop, or maybe a throw of the marbles, and the little girl of the coalman used to sometimes bring me out the dinner her little brother had left! I did not much fancy it, and it was an awful job to be polite and choke it down.

The rest of the streets around were called Little Corn Street, Avon Street and Milk Street. They mostly consisted of Pubs and Rag Merchants, but the top ends were very respectable, they took in lodgers. A Mrs Harris at the top house was very superior, had a nice family of girls, and took in the players of the Theatre and Palace Music Halls from the Sawclose which was near. In Back Street was the slaughterhouses, and on Wednesdays, killing days in the late afternoon when the men had cleared up somewhat, if we had the money we used to queue up to buy the odds and ends for sale. This consisted of a product known as Chitterlings, all pipes full of fat from the pig. I hated it, in fact couldn't digest it, and was always sick. In the cow slaughterhouse we used to get [a] pennyworth or whatever of cows udder, now this was dreadful, like a piece of sponge that wouldn't break. If it was young cattle, I daresay it would be tender enough, but I just couldn't stand it, starving or not. We used to fry it, maybe it should have been boiled, who knows? There comes a time in starvation when one gets past food in a sense, the sight of some would make me vomit, and my mother used to feed me boiled rice with a spoon. Most extraordinary looking back how did I ever recover at all?

One other thing used to happen fairly frequent was the floods. As soon as the river went over the Quay at the back of us, up it came, something dreadful I remember, once it came up to our ceiling, and we were marooned upstairs. The place [was] full of rats and indescribable filth when the waters subsided. I can't recall what happened then about food, but I expect the Salvation Army came around with jugs of soup in boats, they were very good always.

This area had a bad name for fighting and punch ups at weekends, and would be what is known in today's parlance as a 'no go' area. The only ones perhaps the only ones who cared was the Salvation Army, they came every Sunday afternoon on the corner and played the Band, this was one thing that would bring my mother out, so crowds would collect and listen to the Gospel and the singing, 'Rescue the Perishing' 'Who is on the Lord's side?', 'Praise my Soul' etc., etc. I learnt them all. But the pièce de résistance was the girl in the bonnet who played a concertina, how I loved that to see her weaving it about up in the air and down again. I resolved I would play one of those, my biggest ambition, oh me, I never did! I used to think to

myself if only they knew how hungry I was they would give me a piece of bread, but miracles don't happen! Of course, as soon as the collection bag came around we all scattered, and they went to another corner. All the same those bonnet girls were great, every Saturday night calling in every pub selling the 'War Cry'.

These houses were very erratic in size, and some were occupied by whole families and some were let in rooms. Such was number fourteen, the woman with the big family Mrs Perrett occupied the downstairs, and above them lived a couple, Mr and Mrs Walt Holley. Of all the people who passed and repassed me sitting on the pavement, she was the only one who really took pity on me and invited me up to their abode. I think they had one fairly large room as there were other tenants first floor back and up above. The husband was bedridden, paraplegic, what was the cause or how he had come to be like this, I was too young to know. All I know they were most kind, letting me sit by their fire and sharing what food they had.

There was very little charitable institutions at that time, but various religious denominations did good work, and the idea was to get the poor to sign the pledge, that was the beginning as so much drunkenness prevailed and the resultant neglect of children and home life in general. This couple used to be visited by members of the Men's Class from Manvers Street Baptist Chapel, and I used to sit and listen and one of these visitors took me to the class once. His name was Mr Willoughby, his everyday occupation was a 'Paddy' man, this meant he called on all the poor with clothes and you paid whatever you could weekly. He was of course choosey who he gave credit to and knew everybody and all their business, and the usual payment was a shilling a week on a man's suit, the price was usually about twelve shillings and upward. It didn't matter in the least if it all landed up in the pawnshop every Monday morning, it was the usual thing. The queue used to line up before they opened at Mr Newmans pawnshop on the bottom end of St James's Parade at the end of Great Corn Street. You weren't supposed to be served if under a certain age, but I used to go, not with any clothes but my mother's wedding ring, and I remember my head did not come over the top of the counter. I did not care a lot for the lady behind the counter, she was very nosey, and I was conscious she knew too much about me. One was given a hard small cardboard ticket with the date stamp and valuation on it, and one brought this ticket back to redeem the goods at the weekend. The ring was usually redeemed every week when we got the Army Allowance, such a silly procedure!

'The rest of the streets around were called Little Corn Street, Avon Street and Milk Street. They mostly consisted of Pubs and Rag Merchants, but the top ends were very respectable, they took in lodgers. A Mrs Harris at the top house was very superior . . . and took in the players of the Theatre and Palace Music Halls from the Sawclose which was near.' (Picture shows Avon Street c. 1900)

'The queue used to line up before they opened at Mr Newman's pawnshop on the bottom end of St James's Parade at the end of Great Corn Street. You weren't supposed to be served if under a certain age, but I used to go not with any clothes but my mother's wedding ring, and I remember my head did not come over the top of the counter.'

So I went to this class but was so surprised it was all men, and I didn't go again. The idea behind this was to get children 'saved' when young. There was usually a bit of bribery, being in the form of a cup of tea and a bun, food was the great bait, and the families who joined either [with them] the Salvation Army did improve in their way of life. They were helped to find jobs and improved materially, but of course it was hard to keep

on the straight and narrow way, and a good many fell by the wayside. This couple were 'converted and saved', but he used to have the surreptitious bottle of beer, and I remember what a scramble there used to be to hide under the clothes in his bed when chapel people called. Her name was Lizzie and she was my best friend. They bred canaries and the room used to be continual bursts of song, and we used to have to visit potential

'When the odd halfpenny came my way I used to go round the various shops in Southgate Street low end. There was Weeks and Graham, a large shop, a Post Office on the corner where we got our Allowance, and then lower down was Budgets. The biscuits were mostly dust and crumbs done up in the usual funnel blue sugar paper bags.'

customers carrying the bird in small boxes (she was later killed in the Bath blitz in 1942). How I enjoyed these outings, she always had money and would buy me sweets or we would have fish and chips out of newspaper, it was great. The only thing was I was to be sure and not let on and tell 'Walt'.

When the odd halfpenny came my way I used to go round the various shops in Southgate Street low end. There was Weeks and Graham, a large shop, and a Post Office on the corner where we got our Allowance, and then lower down was Budgets. The biscuits were mostly dust and crumbs done up in the usual funnel blue sugar paper bags. Also in Peter Street was a family named Hughes (son now in Kingsmead Square). Manny Hughes, as she was known, sold the 'Pinky Fruit', or would give you some, seldom was a child refused a bruised apple or half rotten orange.

There was too always a shortage of fuel. One could buy 'briquets', a block of solidified small coal, if one couldn't afford half bags or quarter bags of coal. I used to get up early as I felt ashamed of being seen and go around all the ash buckets near, and anything burnable I could find. We burnt the bed once, made of a material called 'milpuff', it stank something awful, not because of dirtiness, but the type of material like wadding and made an awful smoke. Some days some of the kids would rush around the streets carrying sacks and shout 'shavings up' such a scramble you never saw, we all grabbed any bags or sacks handy and rushed around to Longs factory, not far away, and collected the shavings under and around the machines. How these kids knew I could never fathom but I followed the crowd but did not like the noise of the factory, and being so small had a job dragging the sacks. The pork butcher in Southgate Street was named Spears, and a very good shop it was. Here one could get a penny worth of bacon rinds. It incorporated [a] certain amount of fat and bits which could be rendered down and made nice, tasty dripping, if one was lucky enough to have any bread!

One Sunday, when Bath had a large quota of wounded soldiers stationed in various camps and hospitals around, a couple of the older girls took me for a walk. They were out for 'pick ups', I knew quite well what they were up to, but [felt] very important to think they wanted my company, me nine years old and so tiny! One knew the soldiers by the blue uniform they wore. I didn't want to stay with them all the same. When we were going by Bladwells shop, on the corner of the quay, I spotted a lovely piece of bread in the gutter. So I had to get away from these somehow, and I made some excuse, and

went back, and to my great delight the bread was still there. I rushed home with it, and we had the most delicious toast we'd ever tasted with the scrapings of the bacon fat cup! Another product Spears sold was a concoction of pieces called 'Greaves'. One could get a halfpenny worth, it was like scrumpy skin and pieces of dried up meat bits. I supposed all the fat had been extracted and this was the residue. It is now sold for Dogs and Cats! Surprising what one can live and thrive on!

Since those days I have often thought of the prisoners of war and refugee camps, how much worse off were they! Also there was [a] shortage of sugar and therefore no sweets. I believe we had ration books alright, but what [they] obtained I can't recall. There was saccarhin in place of sugar for any cocoa or tea, and it was nasty, always gave me a bad stomach, little tiny white tablets. On the market too was a thing called margarine, Blue Band in place of any butter, this didn't worry me, never had any anyway. What I did have, if I ever managed to get a halfpenny, was a long bean, called a 'locust bean', just like the French type of bean of today, only hard and brown, and very sweet. One just chewed away and chewed away on it as they were rather hard. They are now sold today in the Health Food Stores, and [are] known as 'Carob Beans' or 'St Johns Bread'.

Chapter 5

In the summers after the floods there would be out-breaks of Diptheria and Scarlet Fever, and the fever van would sometimes have half of a family inside. How I wished I could get it!

So 1917 passed, and an odd letter [came] from 'somewhere in France' for us, and sometimes two or three weeks together, which was read and re-read, and carried around by myself as I was so lonely. Some houses fared much worse. They had Telegrams or missives from the War Office saying [a] son or husband was 'missing presumed killed'. One sorrow was everybody's sorrow and everybody helped and sympathised. In spite of the odd rows they were all the best of friends in times of trouble, and everyone knew everybody's business, some of the families being established in the area for many years.

Food was terribly scarce, and the floods continued with the resultant filth and rats, and then one day, out of the blue, my step father came home. Such rejoicing on my part I well remember to think he had got through the bombs and bullets. What I didn't know was how wise he had been, after being in the trenches and seen the carnage and resultant injuries, and having a wounded knee the first time, he had been in the camp as a 'batman' to various officers, and had been in clover. [He] had had good food and done alright. He was horrified at the 'hovel' and the conditions generally. He had got this place in the winter of the year they were married, accommodation being hard to find and not realising how bad it was. He found another little house in a different district on the other side of the river and further up, a part of Bath I had visited only once before with Lizzie Holly to deliver a canary. Here I was accepted by the community, [it was] different having a man to be seen. It was Utopia, three rooms and nice and light, windows on to the narrow cobbled street, there was a gas stove and gas for lighting and a [a] ring to boil the kettle on. The kitchen was a halfway basement where the stove was and a lavatory as well! We did not live down there but up in the middle room, and just the one bedroom. This house, too, was two and sixpence a week. It was owned by a grocer on the main street not far away. He was very good to us. I took the rent up every week, and sometimes when in a good mood, he would give me bits of bacon, most useful but very fat, and I have hated the sight and taste of bacon ever since.

We were still short of food, as my stepfather had only a short leave, he saw us moved in and was soon away again. This area was a completely different type to the last one, this was [a] real slum. It was a part known as the Dolemeads, why I never found out, wasn't too far from the country all the same. There were some houses quite uninhabitable, in fact some were just rubble, then one or two good ones, and across the road the same.

It was very noticeable the shortage of men, most of [the houses] were inhabited by women on their own, mostly with children, either having been left in the lurch by men they had lived with, some were genuine war widows, and two in the street had husbands working. Next door to us was a shop rented from the same landlord as us. They had twelve children, the husband was a quiet little man, and did odd job gardening, and she herself was a great knitter and kept all the family in knitted jumpers and socks. Always had knitting with her, the place wasn't too clean, and I seldom bought anything as she wanted to be too friendly, and I was too wary and wise. Across the road, (it was a very narrow street really, called New Street East), was a family of seven, and next to that a family of eight, and so on all down the occupied houses. The one with the eight children was the only one who had a man working, on the railway, and he earned the princely sum of twenty eight shillings a week, which also gave him a 'privilege' ticket, and they could go on the trains at a reduced rate. They were the envy of everyone as they used to go to Weston-super-Mare for the day in the summer, and that was only for the enjoyment of the few. The family of seven had an awful tragedy, the father committed suicide, and the churches and various bodies rallied around and helped all they could. This was not an uncommon occurrence and just another event in our lives.

Some of the women took in soldiers who deserted, usually colonials, Australians were very much in evidence. I remember one young woman, who lived in the little house on the corner, who had a very smart Australian hidden there for quite a long time, but she was rounded on, and the military police came and took him one day. She was very upset, I remember, and some while after she had a baby girl which I used to mind while she went out charring. I wonder if the child ever knew? I don't expect so. I can remember all the names but won't divulge! A good many descendants [are] alive in Bath today.

We were still in the flood level, and [I] got used to seeing the gas stove and objects underwater, but it wasn't as bad as formerly as the house we were [in was] above street level with

three steps up into the main room. Nineteen eighteen saw the bad 'flu epidemic, and one of our main attractions used to be to run from funeral to funeral, and if it was a pauper's funeral without any followers, we would all fall in behind and go part way. There were so many, we'd run back to the next. It was £5 for a decent funeral, horses with plumes and [a] hearse, but a pauper only had one horse and a wooden box affair. When we had bad floods we did well, had jugs of soup brought by the Vicar (the only time we ever saw him, and I don't remember any Sally Army in this area), also we had free coal for drying out the houses. All these houses had mats on the floor made out of sacks and old clothes. We cut the sacks open and laid them flat, and all old rags cut in small strips were used, just pushed through with a funny hook needle, and one kept on ad infinitum. Couldn't understand it at first and then I found out, it was because of the continual damp seepage from the river. In the summers after the floods there would be outbreaks of Diptheria and Scarlet Fever, and the fever van would sometimes have half of a family inside. How I wished I could get it! I never did which I put down to the fact that we always lime washed the basement after the floodings. The children used to come back looking so fat and well, a fever hospital stay usually meant a long one, and the lovely food they had, jellies and blancmange, and as much as they wanted! I was so upset over this and did my best to catch it but no luck!

One job I had to do, as I seemed to know my way around more than some, was everytime there was a confinement, and this was pretty often, I was sent to Rivers Street Nursing Home. Here I had to give a half a crown and the name and address, and ask for a 'layette'. This would be on loan for a month for all new babies, and then I would return it to get the money back. I suppose it was clothes given to midwives by better off people for the poor. The layettes were large parcels and contained all the necessities for the new baby.

I think about this time must have been the beginnings of the 'Welfare State'. The R.R.P.C.C. started to visit those poor areas. It was a man I did not like, all he did was to pull up my clothes, whether it was to see if I had knickers on or whether he wanted to see the female body I know not. What I do know is he only did it once, and whenever I heard or saw him in the area, I scarpered and quick. There was a lot of illness amongst these large families, of course the word contraception had not been invented, or Marie Stopes ever heard of, not in those parts, there was Rheumatic Fever, this was the most prevalent illness which I suppose was due to so much damp.

Apart from the flooding and continual dampness from that, most of the women took in washing. There were no washing machines as we know them either. One woman who did a huge lot of laundry for a lot of the big houses had a big wooden contraption like a drum and a big stick to manipulate. I never did discover how it worked, but she had a family and they had a hard life. She was a genuine widow, but I don't think there was any allowance, if so very small I'd say. All the days of the week, children would be seen staggering with these big laundry baskets, one each side. Some did the Bear Flat district, which wasn't too far from the Dolemeads, and others did Lansdown area, away up the top of the town, and others did Pulteney Street and Bathwick. The mothers also did charring in some of these houses, sixpence an hour now, not sixpence for a morning like my mother in 1909 and 1910.

The other illnesses amongst the young were Epilepsy and St Vitus's Dance, but of course the worst thing was Rickets, and so many children were knockneed and bow legged, and the word Vitamins was never heard of. So of course death was a frequent visitor, and there were no Funeral Parlours, the deceased if young had a nice, white coffin, and was on a table usually in the same room where the family lived. The age of death was usually between two and three years old, just Bronchitis they'd say, and then dead! The coffin would be left open until the night before the funeral, and we would all go for the last peep and pay our condolences to the parents. Then the crowd would follow to either Locksbrook Cemetery or St

James usually on the Lower Bristol Road, just like in Ireland today. When the motor hearses first came in, and it was not convenient for neighbours to follow on foot, horror was expressed, 'hurrying people off the face of the earth like it', wasn't decent!

I remember a very pretty little girl dying of T.B. (that too was very much in evidence), and we went as a class and said the poem from Longfellow around the 'beir', and of course we always took flowers, wild ones usually picked in Victoria Park or on the common:

> And the mother gave in tears and pain,
> The Flowers she most did love;
> She knew she would meet them all again
> In the fields of light above.
> O not in cruelty not in wrath,
> The Reaper came that day;
> 'Twas an angel visited the green earth,
> And took our flower away.

Chapter 6

I don't know how I came to be inveigled into going to Sunday School as I had no belief in God, my mother had taught me prayers very early, and I always said 'Gentle Jesus' before I slept, but it wasn't real. How could there be a God when I was always so hungry, and when I had prayed so hard in former days, and no food turned up, unless I pinched it?

So the war to end all wars ended, and economically things got worse. My stepfather was demobbed some time in 1919, and had a pension of one pound a week, which was really a munificent sum. Unfortunately, his drinking habits got worse, he couldn't rest until all was spent. He used to drink a beer known as India Pale Ale, it was eight pence a pint, and he was also a 'hail fellow well met' type, and would treat all and sundry. The Secretary of the British Legion, where my stepfather used to frequent, begging more or less, did all he could to help him, and got him various jobs, but they didn't suit. One was at Aldridge and Rankin, a steel works, that didn't last only a few days, too hard! Then the road sweeping job, but he wasn't having that again. Another job was at the Roman Bath going around all the different departments with the towels, that didn't last long either.

So our feeding habits became very sparse again in consequence. I was not too bad as I was still in receipt of the school dinners. The numbers had swelled tremendously by now where it had only been a dozen or two in 1916 at the start, was now a big crowd done in relays. I was a real introvert, but I could join in here with most of the families, and was always in with the crowd especially if anything was going free, such as the Bun Fights, as they were known, at the Mission Hall around the corner. In those days, it was always the done thing to go to a Sunday School of sorts. There wasn't any church in the immediate district. There was Widcombe Baptist Chapel, with a nice Pastor named Mr Huntley in charge, but that was only for posh people who had decent clothes, not for the like of all of us hooligans in the Dolemeads. So some brave people had this Mission Hall with various meetings. One was on Thursday or Tuesday evenings, and the first time I saw the crowd going I tailed on, and asked what is was for, and [was] told it was called The Vanda Vo, and a bun and [an] orange was given away. It was a long time before I discovered it was the 'Band of Hope'. The meeting was in [the] charge of a very nice eccentric type of gentleman known as Mr Willway, to us he was just 'Willow'. It was a rowdy meeting, and I did not go very often, mostly noisy boys, not for me, in spite of the loss of the bun. We were coaxed, cajoled and persuaded to sign the pledge which most of us did. We were all well versed in the problems of drink. It was the curse of so many homes, and pubs were far too numerous, one every five houses, beer brewed mostly on the premises.

We used to sing rousing hymns, that's what I liked! 'Dare to be a Daniel, dare to stand alone', 'Onward Christian soldiers', and such like. I don't know how I came to be inveigled into going to Sunday School as I had no belief in God, my mother had taught me prayers very early, and I always said 'Gentle Jesus' before I slept, but it wasn't real. How could there be a God when I was always so hungry, and when I had prayed so hard in former days, and no food turned up, unless I pinched it? Also hadn't I prayed hard for my mother to be like other kids mothers? But instead she was getting worse. Then hadn't I prayed hard about my stepfather's drink problem, so what was the good telling me of a beautiful Father in heaven? Bunkem, that's all.

Still I went to the Sunday School and learnt the texts and the hymns. It was run, or rather a Superintendant was in charge, named Mr Fred Bladwell. He was a very delicate gentleman, and his wife and their general servant, as the domestics were known as then, all took classes, and my word looking back, what heroes they were. The funny thing was, it didn't matter what chaos reigned, he only used to have to tap the desk a couple of times and quiet would be restored. The boys on one side of the hall and girls the other, their maid took my class for a while, her name was Miss Caroline Quick, and she was a very country person, came from a village called Wiveliscombe in Somerset. We called her 'carry me quick', and tormented her unmercifully, when one remembers how hard she worked. They lived in a large house in the Tyning, Widcombe Hill, and must have scrambled on Sundays to clear up and get down there on foot, none of them had any transport.

Another teacher was named Miss Donaghue, known of course as Hee Haw. She did not vary her theme very much. Her pet saying was, 'Doe ye nexte thynge', always some job to be done however menial. Funny how one remembers! Another character was John, five and twenty four. He was most popular, had a ukelele type of instrument, and taught us choruses, the most known one being:

Praise God it's true
For me and you,
John, five and twenty four.

hence his name. What is John, five and twenty four? Why, verily, verily I say unto you. He that believeth, etc. of course!

It's a marvel how they kept it going all the years they did until Mr Bladwell's death, sometime in the nineteen twenties or maybe early thirties. The part I liked was the singing. We had an Anniversary every June, I don't know what the word meant, but it used to involve a whole four Sundays practice, and we didn't mind that, it meant no texts to be learnt or Bible being read. Then would be the great day, and all parents and friends would be invited, and the Hall would be full. Mine never came, my stepfather when home would usually be tipsy, and my mother's condition was just deteriorating, and she kept in the house more or less all the time. Myself, I went my own way, was out playing all I could, and I suppose trying to make up for the persecution of the past.

It was different here, a man being in evidence. There was a nice playing ground near too, swings and seesaw, the swings upset my stomach, but the seesaw was great. Another diversion was the trains. They would stop at the top of the arch at the river end of the street, and we would chant, 'please throw us a copper', and the halfpennies would come showering out of the trains, especially from the Soldiers. They were in evidence a long time as it took a long time to get organised after a war and get demobbed. A lot of the money fell in the river, and on August Mondays, the river would be lowered and some of the boys would go down in all the mud to find what they could. I had to keep on the outskirts of all these 'melees', as I was so small and would have been injured, however I used to be lucky on occasions. The trains were very near the backs of the houses, and it took a bit of getting used to, the shunting going on all night and the smuts. Curtains used to be filthy in no time, all the same, most people were quite house proud, and used to vie with one another with the nice curtains, the wallpapering, and the continual rag rugs.

About this time, I took bouts of Tonsilitis, and the governess made arrangements for me to go into the Hospital, and be operated on by a Mr Forbes Fraser. He was one of the best of those days, [and] there is a small Hospital named after him. The Hospital in the Centre of the town is now I believe a College. I was in Victoria Ward first, and it was marvellous, I had a sore throat for a few days that was all. The thing was I had lovely food, large bowls of bread and milk, especially. The nurses used to feed me, I remember, as I wolfed things at such a rate. Also, I was kept in for much longer than the usual Tonsil period, and was put in a small ward upstairs, called the Matthew Dixon. Such a lovely time I had, and I really loved the nurses, one in particular, nurse Allen. When I was sent home I was very upset and used to go and sit hours in a little street at the back of the Hospital, where I could smell the ether and other smells of Hospitals. I crotcheted a little table mat, and took [it] in for a present to my beloved nurse, but the man at the desk wouldn't let me in. he took it. I don't suppose she ever got it! It was as black as the ace of spades with my dirty hands, but it was a real labour of love.

Then when I was home just a few days, the governess came for me to go to a Sanatorium, wasn't I excited! It was dreadful to come home to the slums and slipshod ways after the lovely time I'd had in Hospital. Someone went with me on the train, I vaguely remember, and took me to a huge building, right at the end of the sea front. It was called the Royal West of England Sanatorium, and one half was for women, and the other half for men. What was more, this was my first glimpse of the sea, and it was November, I was frightened to death at first, huge great waves, one after another, it took a bit of getting used to. There was another little girl sent from Brierley Hill, some place near Birmingham she told me, she was really delicate. I was much more hardy than she was. We had a great fortnight together, used to have sea water baths twice a week, and again such lovely food, that suited me. When the fortnight was up, or nearly so I began to worry. I did not want to go back to the slum and the drink and my weird mother, so I devised a plan to make myself ill so that I could stay! I used to shut myself in the corridor and go around and around to make myself giddy because I knew then I might be sick. Did they see through my wiles I wonder, anyway I was overjoyed when I was allowed to stay another fortnight. The other little girl went home but I was very happy. I used to go all along, right to the old pier and back, except when the weather was too bad. The women were mostly elderly workers from Wills Tobacco factory at Bristol. We used to have concerts and singsongs, 'Roses of Picardy', and 'If you were the only girl in the world', all the war songs. Like all good things, it came to an end, and I nearly broke my heart, but one had to face up to it and that was it.

Life wasn't all bad, I still had the school dinners and my friend Miss Roach. The next year a scheme was started for deprived children to have [a] holiday in the country near Bath. believe it was for three weeks during the summer holidays, and

I was one of the chosen ones. Here Miss Roach showed her practicality, and had me at her house for a weekend. She lived in Kipling Avenue on the Bear Flat. She rigged me out in two complete outfits. I was still so dirty, after all I was only thirteen and not like girls of that age today, I was very immature, and never [had] any money for clothes, we never had enough for food. I had two lovely Welsh flannel blouses, and [a] pinafore skirt and nice underclothes, all these clothes were given by better off parents of the school. My weekend there was spoilt by another girl who had been in a similar position as myself whom the governess had adopted. She was intensely jealous and tried to upset me. Her mother had gone to gaol over drinking and child neglect. Also there was a very playful Tabby pussy named Dinah. She was very wild and chased me, and the little dog was lovely, named Becky after someone in a book [called] Vanity Fair.

So I went on the train with a lot of other kids, with our clothes in paper parcels. This was a different holiday, and I did not like it one bit. There were three of us billeted on an elderly couple, named Mr and Mrs Gale, and the village was called Gastard. Here we picked blackcurrants and did odd jobs, the like of which I'd never done and didn't want to do. You see I was from a town, and there was always some diversion and people about. Here it was very lonely, and the couple were too old really. Also the two girls with me were sisters, and I was out of everything. I was glad when the three weeks was up, and I could go home. Most children had someone to meet them, not me! Oh no, here I was again on the platform looking in vain for someone glad to see me. However, I met my stepfather on my way home, not quite blind drunk as the saying goes, but nearly. I remember I burst into tears at the ignominy and injustice of it all, and then when I got home, my mother was soaking her feet of all things, and not a sign of food. What a welcome, I remember thinking.

Until now, I had more or less run wild, no one cared, and I was glad to be out of the house as much as I could. I was usually made welcome in most houses to play, or more often than not to mind the inevitable new babies, and I just went home more or less to sleep. Wednesday was the pension day, our only income, and this was usually disposed of in the pub, and our next source of income was the pawnshop. One day, when my stepfather was short of money for more beer, he used to have a bad hangover next day, and always as he said 'wanted a hair of the dog that bit him', and had to have it somehow. He sent my mother to the pawnshop with his boots, and she was gone an

awful long time, and as he raved over the pubs being shut before she got back, wasn't there a knock at the door and a policeman stood there with the boots under his arm. I nearly fainted with fright, and for years after always went as white as a sheet, as the saying goes, if a knock came at the door. It seems my mother was acting very strange and was arrested. I never did hear the details, and she was committed to Wells Asylum.

Here she stayed for fifteen years, dying at the age of 48 of Consumption. What happened was my stepfather had got his weekly pension (it was a Wednesday), and had spent it on drink as was his usual wont. The trouble was he didn't have any money left for the evening drinking session, and sent my mother to the pawnshop with his boots with the dire result (of her 'arrest'). My job was to watch him while she was gone, as he was often setting the sofa on fire with his inability to light his pipe, being so drunk. Ever saw anyone with a match or lighted paper trying to light a pipe? Highly entertaining, but dangerous.

Chapter 7

So it was no work, no food, so I had to try my best to earn a couple of shillings. . . . I only did two hours every morning, again five shillings a week, and I stayed there three and a half years! My elevenses consisted of a cup of hot water with a lump of dripping in it.

So I had an excuse to leave school. School wasn't very enforced anyway, true there were Inspectors going around after truants, but it was only a farce, and no-one ever took much notice, especially if there was a fairly good reason such as mine was. I had to keep house, I said, and that was the end of my schooling. When I was at Kingsmead School, I must admit I was very happy, at least as happy as any child can be, in spite of such dreadful home surroundings, and what little knowledge I had was acquired in the couple of years [spent] there on and off. At least I could read very well, and write after a fashion, but the arithmetic foxed me. With reference to Geography or History, and or Grammar, I had only the haziest ideas.

The splitting up of schools was about 1919/1920, and I was 11, something to do with the 11 plus? I was transferred to Weymouth House at Abbey Green, near old Mr and Mrs 'Fishy' Evans fish and chip shop. They were a nice couple and had a good business, next door almost to the man who mended the kettles, and around the corner was a China repairer who mended broken china for a few coppers, [in] Swallow Street, I think. Also Titley's Grocer's warehouse where one went for a ½d worth of salt. He had a great big block, and would cut off a good piece. The Weymouth House School was quite a disaster, big, crowded classes and a most peculiar headmistress. She fell in 'love', I believe, with the Headmaster of the boys section, a Mr Arnold, and was dismissed, or went queer, I don't know which. I had left by this time [in] the early 1920s.

There was no such thing as dole, although I think it was to come in fairly soon. We had my stepfather's small pension for a while, but this didn't last very long because he wasn't considered sufficiently incapacitated, one had to have great disability to get £1 a week. However, there was a scheme for 2 days work a week for ex-soldiers, whereby they were allowed 10/-, i.e. five shillings (25p) a day. All the same, my stepfather had a very plausible way with him, and went to various ex-army schemes, which were helping such men. One very good friend

of his was the Secretary of the British Legion. He was a very nice man, always giving up clothes, which went straightway to the Pawnshop, and then to the pub, and that was my life. So it was no work, no food, so I had to try my best to earn a couple of shillings.

My first job was looking after someones baby, while she, (the mother, Mrs Cashnella in Claverton Street) was convalescing, and I earned 1/- a day plus a certain amount of food, not much but [it] was something. The husband himself was an ex-soldier, and only [had] a small pension, so that didn't last long, they just couldn't afford it. About this time, my 'dad' got friendly with a fellow drinker, and used to visit their house. It was a row of Coachmans cottages, or gardeners cottages, with nice long gardens in the midst of the big houses on Bathwick Hill. This man's wife, Mrs Edith Coles, was her name, was one of the kindest and best friends I ever had. She was a most lovely cook, and was always out working, and I'm sure she must have thought me an awful nuisance, but I amused their one and only girl, Kathleen, and kind of looked after her, as she was very delicate, and a couple of years younger than myself. Mrs Coles got me a job in one of the houses she worked in, an architect, the gentleman was, a Mr Mowbray Greene. I am afraid I was very undisciplined and most unhappy. I was really very fond of my stepfather, and as I had to live in, and the horrible bedroom, a big attic and bare boards, no it was not for me, and I just ran home after about five days, and my 'dad' had to go and retrieve my little tin trunk and its belongings. However, it did not break my friendship with dear Mrs Coles. She gave me the odd meal, and showed me how to cook, I had a lot to thank her for.

About this time, 1921 or thereabouts, the big houses were giving up the coaches and horses and were acquiring cars, so meant the coachmen learning to drive or being sacked. There was a big house up above the Coles' cottage, and I believe the gentleman had died. [It is] now a Salvation Army Home, I believe, Oakwood. Anyway, there was great consternation amongst the staff, especially the coachmen and gardeners. Next to Mrs Coles', at no. 1 Windsor Terrace (now a swanky, new Terrace, I believe), at no. 2, was one of these coachmen, and his father had branched out and got himself a Taxi. The father was one of the pioneers of the Bath Taxi Rank. He had a real, queer affair, and was one of the sights. It was a taxi alright, with a big basket on top. He was a very nice man, and took all the ribbing about his chariot in good part. He was a real Irishman, named Joe Ryan, and lived at Richmond Place, Beacon Hill. It was his son, Joe, who lived next to Mrs Coles. They had two small babies, Patrick and Michael respectively and his wife had been a nanny in some big, private family, and found she had her hands full after her life of nursery maids etc., so I was asked if I would like the job of looking after these two for five shillings a week, and some meals, which of course I jumped at. Mrs Ryan had been given the family perambulator when she had her first baby, well such a pram! Some difference to today's little affairs. It was called a 'Dunkeley', such a huge contraption, my head came level with the handlebars, so you can imagine my struggle pushing this up Bathwick Hill with two babies, one 18 months and the other very young. Didn't matter which way one went it was up, and my usual walk was down along Cleveland Walk. Anyway, we were glad of the money, but like the other, it didn't last long. The Taxis weren't doing too well, or anything else either. This was the beginning of the big slump, and that was it.

My next job was passed on to me by one of the women in the Dolemeads. Most [of them] went out 'charring', and this was a job too many for this one. So I went to a house in Pulteney Gardens, belonging to a Mr and Mrs Wood and his daughter. It was the second wife, and it was not exactly a 'happy' home. They were belonging to a sect known as the Exclusive Brethren, and had a meeting room in New King Street, called Cumberland Hall, now a Christadelphian Meeting Room. The Brethren had a 'division', and this one lot took a room elsewhere. This was left to just a few elderly ones who let it deteriorate in an alarming state. They were mean and make no mistake. I only did two hours every morning, again five shillings a week, and stayed there three and a half years! My elevenses consisted of a cup of hot water with a lump of dripping in it. Ugh, it made me vomit, so I politely refused it after a couple of mornings. The daughter was very kind, but was found out giving me a couple of potatoes or some little thing, and words would ensue!

However, the second Mrs Wood got tired of the area and wanted a house nearer her mother in Oldfield Road, and they bought a lovely large house in Wells Road. Whether it was carrying buckets and goods from Pulteney Gardens to Wells Road or whatever, but I took an awful illness, bleeding from the kidneys, and so left. I was home for six months, ill and very anaemic. At the end of the six months, my 'Panel money' was finished. This was the equivalent of today's health service. At the end of these six months payments, one had to visit a doctor in the hospital to see if one could still be eligible for a reduced amount. This marvellous gentleman said I was well enough for a nice, light job, and not on any account to do any domestic work or such like again, such twaddle. It was a case of doing what one could get, especially being so illiterate and uneducated. So I took in sewing and knitting. Well, you can just imagine in a poor district where people had little money for bread let alone sewing! However, I earned a sixpence here and a shilling there. My chief job was to make kids clothes out of old grown up things. I just dread to think what sometimes the end result must have been. The knitting was the worst paid. A cardigan, maybe, I could get 1/6 (7½p), and woe betide me if I got a pattern wrong.

All this time, I was keeping house as best I could with my boozie stepfather. Not that he was always drunk, but he was a real alcholic, would go two or three weeks without and then break out, and would be drunk for 3 or 4 days. [He would] sell and pawn everything he could lay his hands on and sell the pawn tickets so I could never get anything back. My worst grief was a nice, new blue coat what I'd got, and came home and it was gone. It was a hopeless situation, and how I kept any mental balance I can't think. I know I was near suicide several times.

However, I got a job cleaning Axford and Smith's offices. They were builders, and the offices were at the bottom of Widcombe Hill. I had a shilling a morning of 2 hours from 7 am till 9 am, and while I was there didn't I drop lucky, and our landlord, Harrison, who kept a grocer shop near there in Widcombe Parade, offered me the job of cleaning the flat above the shop. This was real money, 7/6 a week for 2 hours, five mornings a week, so with the two jobs I was doing well. I always felt the need of a sewing machine, as I was still asked to do sewing jobs, and there was a second hand shop at the top of our street. It was kept by a nice man called Mr Rosenburg, and he let me pay a shilling a week towards an old treadle machine. It was a very good investment, 17/6 in all, and earned me many a meal. The Rosenburg family were very good, one went to Jersey, growing tomatoes, and made an amount of money, and very generously gave or left money for St Johns Hospital old people, and there is a lovely, new block named after him, Rosenburg House in Westgate Buildings.

Then things [in the] economy got worse, so about 1928 my job gave out, couldn't afford it. So back I went to the knitting anything I could get. One temporary job I got one Christmas was at a big house called the Cloisters, now made into several houses, it was at Perrymead. Well, it was a most beautiful big

35

hall, the original one when it was a 'Cloister', I think. It was a big Christmas dinner, and I was scared stiff, I'd never been in or seen such grandeur. I'm afraid my help was not a lot of good, I was so small and couldn't reach to clear the plates quickly enough. How I got through it and the washing up I can't remember, but I had a nice parcel of leavings to bring home!

About this time, I also did a temporary live-in job at a big house at Lansdown, called Stoneleigh, cook general, come all sorts while the maids had holidays. They were very pleased with me although I say it [myself]. It was a Major and Mrs Wade, and son and daughter. Major Wade was badly wounded in the 1914 War, and had a false plate in his face. It was not really noticeable, but very painful at times. They bred scottie dogs, and I was very friendly with the kennel maid for the rest of her life. We went to Scotland once to the kennel maid's house. [They were] very affluent farmers in Huntly, Aberdeenshire. The Wades afterwards moved to Box Ashley, and sold Stoneleigh, which I believe has now been converted into a hotel. Mrs Wade was a lovely lady and lived to a great age, and always kept in touch with me. Unfortunately, they lost their only son, Mr Tony, in the Burmese campaign in 1942. Miss Peggy Wade is now, I believe, one of the chief guides at the American Museum. [She] was doing the gingerbread in 'Conkey's Tavern' [there] not very long ago.

Chapter 8

I must have looked a pretty pitiful sight in my shabby clothes, and so cold. The lady looked [at] me over her pince-nez, and said the job is filled I'm afraid.

Then came 1929, January, bitterly cold, frost and ice, and still no work, and ten shillings a week 'parish' money. Although my Dad still did an odd day's gardening or caddying on the golf course, not much of that went into housekeeping. I won't say how many jobs were obtained for him by various charitable bodies, and how he always lost them through drink, or how 'it was much too hard', or 'too far', he was a pastmaster at work dodging. However, one evening, a kindly neighbour sent me the local paper with a job vacancy for someone to wash up, and although it was late evening, I decided to try for it. It was in a hotel I vaguely knew, but I was a long time getting there because of the ice and cold. I was very timid when I saw this grand place, all bright lights, and the office was through a large lounge, the like of such I'd never seen before, deep carpet and lovely furniture, and a huge fire, and all posh people, sitting, drinking out of dolls cups, and whatever that was for I couldn't think. Why the office was through the lounge I can't think either, unless it was [so] the manageress could watch staff through one window, and visitors through the other. Now it is modernised and [has] a proper reception [in the] usual style of today.

I must have looked a pretty pitiful sight in my shabby clothes, and so cold. The lady looked [at] me over her pince-nez, and said the job is filled I'm afraid. I suppose my face showed my disappointment, but she said, I'll have your name and address, and I'll know when I need someone the next time. That was it, disappointment again. However, about 9 o'clock the next morning, didn't an important looking man in livery come to the door and say if I liked to go back with him to see the lady again, she thought she had a little job that might suit me! Well, didn't that open my mind to another world, my goodness! Mrs Pratt, for that was [the name of] the hotel had evidently felt sorry for me, and made a little job for me to help an elderly chambermaid, who was not too good at stairs, (there were no lifts then). So this I was delighted to do, I had to fetch her trays and do the bathrooms on her floor, and then a couple of nights a week, take a turn washing up in what was called a 'Stillroom', why I never found out. A noisier place one could never imagine, waiters rushing about and cluttering all the silver into various receptacles, and plates, and such chaos, I'd never seen.

One thing, I did well off the plates. These visitors were all in Bath Spa, as it was known, for the 'treatment'. How they used to wade all down the menus, such a list of food I'd never heard of, let alone seen. First it was little bits, pieces called 'Hors d'ouvres' and then a lovely big piece of fish, either done in crumbs or steamed with sauces of various kinds, followed by choice of joint, then choice of sweet, followed by a little savoury, and then cheese and biscuits. After this repast, they would all retire to the aforesaid lounges and smoke room, and drawing room with the dolls cups, which I learnt contained coffee, and a lot had liquers with that as well. Why, bless my soul, I thought, fancy, no wonder they were fat and wanted treatment!

All the same, it was a completely new environment, and I could never get to work quick enough. Remember, it was a dreadful depression time between 1929 and 1933, especially so I knew there were others ready to take my place if I didn't do my best. Of course, I didn't have the foggiest idea about vacuum cleaners, or how a tray was laid, but I soon learnt believe me. All that throw out food kept us well and we did alright. Also, I occasionally got a half a crown tip, or maybe more, and I will say the old chambermaid was never jealous, and used to put me in the visitors area when they were departing. Needless to say, I got better in health and stronger for the better food, and above all I used to save what I could, unbeknown to Dad, the less he knew about money the better. My wages were 7/6 a week for every morning, 3 or 4 hours, and several evenings for the washing up relief. They used to have about 80 visitors when full. The Bath season for treatment was the first week in September till [the] end of April, and when it began to get warm, as Bath is in such a hollow, it could be warm in summer.

My Dad still got drunk, and I got very fed up when I saw what a good time the girls had, and how swanky they dressed, went out to dances, and such a different life to mine. So I evolved a plan to get him away, and paid my dad's fare to his brother in Birmingham, he was always talking about, and got him to go there, as a girl chambermaid got married, and Mrs Pratt offered me her 'floor', the first floor of ten rooms. It was selfish, as I was so lonely and [had] had no personal affection. I only had him to cling to, and we used to go to visit Mother in the Asylum one afternoon a week, but I got so fed up with him getting drunk each time, and me having to hold him by the hand as he was so unsteady, so that part of my life I decided to end, and to live in.

Thus it was ten rooms, responsible for so much under a housekeeper and hard work. Visitors for treatment usually came for three weeks, and in the winter we had our 'permanents'. These were people who came back every year at a reduced rate usually Bath was not a tourist attraction like today. The first coach loads of Americans came about 1934 or 5, I think, and the hotels felt it was humiliating to take such people as 'one nighters', and I remember at the posh Empire Hotel, the coaches had to go around the back at [the] Police Station, where [the] Guildhall is now, as it was so demeaning. It soon got common enough, and hotels were glad enough to welcome them, and are now.

What a revelation it was to me, seeing well educated, and really nice, aristocratic people, and some of course, not so nice! I had some lovely rooms to look after, first floor south, one was the room (or supposed to be) which Sir Walter Scott was in when he lived in South Parade. My clients varied tremendously. Some were very difficult and cranky, so I always had to be very diplomatic, an art I soon learnt. You would soon be out of a job if you were reported for being rude, or maybe the slightest thing, some of them were very autocratic. Several long stayers I remember well. Poor old Miss Hayter, nearly blind, and no relatives, or ever any visitors. I still have a work bag she gave me one Christmas. When she died, the relatives were numerous, came up from the ground, I think. Then, next door was Mrs Parry Jones, a very elderly lady, great friend of Mr and Mrs Fred Weatherby. He was a very clever man, but is remembered for his songs, 'We've just come up from Somerset', and best of all, 'Danny Boy'. He is buried in Smallcombe Churchyard, now called Bathwick, and his widow stayed at Pratts with Mrs Parry Jones for company for a long while. She suffered dreadfully from asthma, and I had to light a saucer of incense, or some such stuff for inhalation, every night. Mrs Parry Jones had a glass eye, and I had to poke it out very carefully every night with a hairpin, and put it in a small glass of fluid made special. I shall never forget the feeling almost of horror to see this glass eye in my hand looking at me, [but] one soon got used to it. Also, she used a commode, and always left a 1/- (5p) on top when [she] had been obliged to use it. I must emphasise the fact that none of the rooms had toilets or bathrooms, [there were only] two bathrooms and loos on each floor. Wouldn't do for today would it? All the rooms had coal fires, and jugs and basins, so coal had to be carried, and cans of hot water. Then there was Mr Adair in no. 6, and Mr Wainwright along the corridor, [and] these were more or less resident. The best ones I liked were the regular treatment people, most came every year for three weeks, some quite young, and looked upon it as a holiday.

This was when I would come into my own and do well. They would usually be so pleased at being cured (yes, there were some marvellous cures, people who came on two sticks and walked out), auto suggestion, or the masseuse, or maybe the nice, attractive consultant? Still, myself, I have great faith in the Hot Spring. Anyway, when the treatment was completed, some of the ladies went to Milsom Street, mostly to Jolly's for a shopping spree, and a nice heap of clothes would be in the waste paper baskets. I got some lovely clothing, in fact, I was well supplied with hats, some Bankok straw or lovely velour ones, which I used to get re-blocked, and shoes, and silk stockings, and occasionally a suit. So I saved my wages and tips, and was getting quite affluent. Also, for the first time, I had holidays, London one year, and Bournemouth the next. Of course, if there was a lady's maid in the entourage, [it was] no good for clothes!

[Also] there were the Conway Thorntons, mother and son, and maid, sometimes [a] chauffeur, also Mrs Rivett Carnac, and such nice people, educated me in many ways. We had some not quite so nice. 'Chippy' Smith I didn't care for (Smith's crisps inventor), [and] plenty of cranky folks too. One was a Mr Arthur Fallows, who gave books and pictures, but never tips, and had a very fussy, Norwegian wife with him. He used to write me letters in a later time, as his wife left him, because I couldn't stop to talk. Some time after he died, I was sent for by the manageress who asked me for my letters. What I didn't know was his wife was contesting his will, and wanted proof of insanity. The gentleman who was there (a solicitor, I presume) assured me I would have them returned, but of course it seems I never did, and also I was mentioned in the will, but I heard no more.

In 1935, my best friend Mrs Pratt died from mastoid, and I suffered dreadful grief, and whereas with her I could do no wrong, with her sister-in-law, who took over the management after her death, I could do nothing right, so things were not pleasant. I had the large sum of £160 saved, so I borrowed £40, and bought myself a little cottage, very poor really, but [with] lovely views, and 1 bedroom, 1 sitting-room, 1 kitchen, and a lovely piece of garden. So that was the happiest years I ever really spent. The girls spoilt me, having known of my past sorrow, and gave me Birthday parties and presents. We worked hard, but that was the custom, [there were] no unions then. I found the cottage very lonely, but got a job [as] daily domestic for the firm of Blackmore and Langdon, the Begonia and Delphinium growers (the Langdon part of the firm), but I missed the Hotel life and company, so I worked there for the winter, and thought I would travel and do what was known as 'season work'. I tried to let my cottage for a short let, but it wasn't quite swanky although I'd got water and electricity, and was quite cosy.

First of all I tried Cafe work because I really was scared of going places alone. I had several 'friends' in Pratts Hotel, but no one really close or of my own turn of mind, so I plodded my own little way. I tried the Cadena Cafe, in what was then Colmers, and was engaged as a waitress, but it seemed one could always get waitresses, but not kitchen or behind the scene workers, and evidently I looked a 'soft touch', or the Supervisor could see I knew the workings of the Catering trade. So I was demoted to the kitchen, at first the Supervisor said only for a day as they were so short of staff, and [they] couldn't be obtained, etc. etc. So I obliged but of course in the Hotels it was always men called kitchen porters who did that sort of work, and it was far too hard and heavy for me being so slight, carrying big, heavy trays, and cleaning dirty, big pots and pans, not my scene after the bedroom and dining room work I had been used to.

So every day I said when was I going into the Cafe, but she always evaded the question with some excuse or other, and at the end of the week I demanded my cards, but she just laughed and said, don't be silly, you do the job very well, and you can have kitchen wages, which was 17/6 a week, instead of the usual waitress wage of 15/-, less 1/6 insurance. It was very busy at that time because the beauty queen of Bath was a waitress there, and people came even if really only for tea to see her. Her name was Barbara Pearce, and she was really lovely, tall and good looking, blue eyes and dark hair type, and such good poise. I remember how I used to envy her a bit. She was a Combe Down girl, perhaps it was the fresh air from the hills [that] gave her such a lovely complexion. However, the Supervisor did not give me my 'cards', which would be an awful handicap in getting another job.

I did not let it worry me too much, but went to the Labour Exchange and explained the situation, and asked if they had any seaside work near Bath, at Weston-super-Mare for instance, and they had, so I shut and barricaded my cottage as best I could, and went for the interview. It was at the Lancaster Hotel, towards the old pier, and they asked me to start straight away, which I did. Bath was only an hour and a half Bus ride away, so I could go on any half day and visit my little cottage and get any clothes. It was a very hard, busy place, and we had to wait for our meals after the visitors had had theirs. I remember, I used to nearly faint by lunch time, 2.30 or later, in fact I got into the habit of getting a 'booster' to keep me going, i.e. some Horlicks Tablets to suck, and they kept me going. I remember the staff well, a cook with marriage problems from across the Channel, she used to go home by steamer, [to] Merthyr Tydfil, South Wales somewhere, and there was a widow from Bath, and a delicate girl from Bristol who shouldn't have been working at all. She died the following year from heart trouble. So I stayed and got a few pounds together, tips and wages, and left in September when [the] season ended. The Hotel was open all the year, but the family ran it themselves, Ma and Pa and Son and Wife. I tell you there's no harder way of earning a living.

This was 1937, and I returned and went back to my daily work for the winter, this time I worked for the other half of the Delphinium Nursery people, Mr and Mrs Allan Langdon at Southdown Lodge, quite a good walk every morning getting there by 8 am. I really hated it, big coal house and boiler to see to, and the cooking to do. They were exceptionally nice people though, and I had quite a job to leave them the next spring as I thought I would try another season job, and set my sights on something better this time, and thought I would try Bournemouth. The Langdons tried all sorts of blandishment to keep me, but I was determined although sorry, as I felt I was being unkind, Mrs [Langdon] being very delicate, and it was difficult just as they got used to one, and then to depart. The former maid had been with them years. Albeit I salvaged my conscience by getting an elderly person I knew to take my job and she did, and lived in and was quite happy there.

However, I'm a bit ahead of things! The job at Weston I hadn't any Insurance Cards, and in the meantime they took my story in good faith, and said the Labour Exchange would get them for me, which happened in a round about way. It seemed the Labour Exchange had taken up my case, re me not getting the job I was promised, and I had to go before a Tribunal. One day, while at Weston-super-Mare, I had a notification to go to a Board Meeting of Officials re my Cards and week's wage, and lo and behold I had this most important document, to say it was a Travel Document to a Tribunal at Taunton, that my day's expenses would be paid, i.e. lunch and any wages lost. I felt dreadfully important I can tell you, and so I found this place at Taunton at the time appointed. And was I scared, I had to go before an awful lot of elderly gentlemen sitting around a large table, poor little me stood at one end, and had to answer questions. However, my courage returned although I was certainly very overawed by the occasion. So I stood up bravely and asked, (in reply to the question why had I left) 'If any of you gentlemen present know what the inside of a large catering establishment was like? I stated I had experience of Hotels for a few years, and in the one I was in a Kitchen Porter always did the work I was asked to do at the Cadena, and [I] was quite unfit to do it, and so I was given a week's wages, and the Cards had already been returned via the Labour Exchange.

In 1938, I tried a better class place this time, one always got the job through the 'Labour', and they gave one a selection to choose from, so I chose the 'Sandbanks', a new Hotel opened on the outskirts of 24 rooms, plus the Bathrooms and Suites which comprised some. My word, this was slavery (wages overall the same 15/- per week), and I found it very hard going. The clients were not the toffs of Bath, but very good money wise. It was Billy Cotton, and jockey Gordon Richards, and such like clients. It was usually a 'fiver' in tips, and mind you this was good money in 1938. It was a very strict Hotel re uniform, and no trespassing on anyone elses territory. In fact, I only saw the Dining Room from the beach. It meant instant dismissal if for any reason you broke the rules, and that's what kept it pretty first class. There was a lovely Ballroom and Swimming Pool. Such things hadn't been heard of before, only perhaps in America. It used to keep us awake in the Staff Wing on dance nights, but one fell into bed so exhausted nothing mattered. Every room was most luxuriously furnished, some blue eyed maple, and some of every different kind of good modern furniture. [It was] owned by [the] Ball family, they also owned the Haven at the end of Sandbanks and one in Swanage, and I think the Burlington in central Bournemouth. [There was] very little off duty [time], but one half day a week from 3 pm. I managed to do a steamer trip around the old Harvy Rocks to Swanage, but mostly I went to the Pictures, and saw Dianna Durban and Snow White, Sailor's Afloat, too, that year, I believe. All in all, I enjoyed it, stayed the full season and came back with the massive sum of £50, which I had saved, and also a good bonus on early Tea Trays, which was a welcome new thing to me.

Chapter 9

When war broke out, I cried my eyes out for days, I was the only one, more or less, who could remember the futility of war, all those maimed young men, and the endless lists of war dead.

So here I came back again to my little cottage with the lovely views and all conveniences to hand. Bus every quarter of an hour to town, Pillar Box on [the] corner, and shop across Mount Road, kept by Mr and Mrs Davis. Took a job now [as] daily in Theobald's Cafe, (now Carwardine's), didn't like it very much really, but stuck it 'till season time came again. I hied me off to Torquay this year, 1939. It was a disaster, the Osborne Hotel [the] worst such place I'd ever been in, beds full of maggots, and kitchen full of the biggest rats I'd ever seen. Unfortunately, the owner, a very nice Colonel, had a manager, and it was a hopeless arrangement, as they say, no one looks after your business like yourself, so it was here. Also, it was a very wet summer, at least until August, and then trade looked up, but then World War II loomed, and all the young men, visitors and staff, were called up. When war broke out, I cried my eyes out for days. I was the only one, more or less, who could remember the futility of war, all those maimed young men, and the endless lists of war dead.

I returned to find Bath more or less taken over by H.M. Government for defence. I did like others, let my cottage for £1 a week, and took a job for my war effort in Horstmann's Gear Works, but did not stay as I was most unsuitable for factory work. I lived with a friend of mine for a while, after her husband, who had been in the Royal Marines was called up, being on their reserve. Eventually, I went back to Hotel work 'till 1942, and then hey presto, all the Hotels were commandeered after the Bath Blitz. Prior to this (April 1942), we had a remarkable experience, owing to the fact that all the male staff in Hotels were called up, we just had to put up with the best we could get, and some of the new ones were completely inexperienced and useless. Bath treatment had gone by the board now, and the Hotels were mostly full of refugees from Nazi Germany, people who were wealthy and wise enough to get out while the going was good. They travelled about from place to place, not knowing where to go, [and] about 1942, they were put into camps or various places. I just don't know what happened. I do know at the Southbourne [Hotel], which was in South Parade, the other side of Pratts, (now flats), we had some very nice German and Austrian people, all good class, singers and jewellers amongst them.

Among the new staff, we had a very peculiar person for a waitress. She would down tools at odd times, and say I'm going off duty now, to our amazement, just as lunch was going to be served or some such awkward time. One day at our meal table, we had a most awful altercation with her, and concluded she was a 'head' case without doubt. Someone happened to mention something derogatory about the Russians or Germans, and she went berserk, saying 'Ah you'll think differently when that Church over the road (St John's R.C.) is in ruins'. and sure enough we thought of her when the raid was on, and we were in the basement, and the most awful crashes above our heads, the china was all over the place off the shelves, and such destruction, yes, it was the church. The authorities were evidently on the alert, however, and she was arrested on Government Property with a male colleague, and was detained during the duration.

[Following the bombing known as the Bath Blitz], I had to walk through mountains of rubble, piles of broken glass, telephone wires down, with the smell of cordite something shocking, to look for my cottage. I expected it to be a pile of rubble, but luckily it was only badly shaken. The other side of Twerton Round Hill got it very badly, and a lot lost lives and were maimed in that area.

Now what to do? I had to give my cottage tenants notice. So back I came and was given a choice of War Work, either on the Buses, or scraping sacks for J. A. Rank at the flour mill in Bristol Road, which they had taken over, being bombed out of the East End of London. I chose sacks, [it was] too giddy for me [on the] Buses. Here was a horrible 'forewoman'. I did not quite come up to her standards, never having scraped sacks before. We had to do a quota of a 100 a day. A lot of these were caked inches thick, having come from army and navy camps

'Following the bombing known as the Bath Blitz, I had to walk through mountains of rubble, piles of broken glass, telephone wires down, with the smell of cordite something shocking, to look for my cottage. I expected it to be a pile of rubble, but luckily it was only badly shaken. The other side of Twerton Round Hill got it very badly....'

and left outside in the rain, and scrape, scrape, scrape, it was no joke. Also, there was a big machine that beat off the big, thick lumps first. A big woman was usually on it, but we had to take a turn. Of course, me being so slight, and it was a powerful machine, I was very nearly dragged into it. The fingers of my right hand have been damaged ever since, but I did not know, nor was I told, that I should have put a claim in for compensation. However, that is only one of my many misfortunes, and has not handicapped me too badly, except now in old age, the arthritic condition. I was here 'till about 1944 or 1945, the war was coming to its close, and as I lived on a bad Bus route, I used to leave a few minutes early, and the forewoman wasn't having that, so I was sacked for the first time in my life. She made up some reason or other, and it meant a Tribunal hearing, but when the interviewer saw me, he dismissed the case, and said for health reasons I could work where I liked.

So back to Cafe work as quick as I could, Theobalds again [but] did not like [it]. Tried [the] Little Kitchen, very nice owner, but most incapable of Restaurant (work). He was a Captain Brooks, army men, yes, but female staff, no! He sold to a private family, who did not want outside help. Across the street I went to Jill's Grill, and this was only lunch time, then home and back at 5.30 'till all hours. Walking home at 1 am was quite usual, and stopping, before I went to bed, to listen to the nightingales at Padleigh Bottom. Are they still there I wonder?

Here with the Admiralty come to Bath, all my acquaintances were getting marvellous jobs with the Government, and kept on to me to try. They were trained, although quite inexperienced to Clerical work of various kinds, and Post Office trained Telephonists, and getting such good money. Why not I said, so I applied, and sat for this examination and the Supervisor was very pleased, my spelling being correct, and I seemed to know about the subject, it was about re-victualling of ships, and a lot of the applicants seemed quite at sea with it. Then came the unthought of, horrible show up again. Would I fill in the necessary forms? Well, one of the first questions was about ones parents! That done it! I couldn't, of course, supply father's name and nationality, done for security reasons, of course, and my Birth Certificate I never showed! Later in life, I got one for Passport purposes, known as a 'Red one'. So that was it, my dreams of an easy post went for a 'Burton', and back to the old grind I had to go, and there I remained 'till 1955, or maybe it was 1956, and Mrs Lake, the owner, sold, and I was out of work.

However, a friend came along and persuaded me to try for her job, as she was leaving, it was evening Telephonist at the Bath and Wessex Orthopaedic Hospital. How I contrived to get it, I'll never know, as I had little or no experience of switchboards, and the workings thereof. I had worked on one now and again, the Hotel ones, and gleaned some idea. The Head, Miss Day, took me on, and it was the best paid and easiest job I'd ever had. It taught me what I had missed by not being educated. Of course, sometimes it was complicated. I had to read out the operation lists sometimes, to the Surgeons, Mr Tom Price, Mr J. Bastow, and Mr Hedley Hall, and others now still there, Mr Bliss and Mr Yeoman, and I must say they were all exceedingly patient with my mispronunciation of Laminectomy, and so forth. And here I stayed 'till December 1966 when I retired.

Previous to this in 1957, I had met and married an Irish widower, and as I was so lonely, it was lovely to have someone to care for. However, in 1964/5, my cottage was compulsorily purchased and I was very grieved, especially by the poor price given. However, we took other accommodation for a year, and as we were both retirement age, we went to his home in Eire for 14 years (in December 1966) and as he died there in 1980, I thought I would come back to my roots! Of the fourteen years spent there? Well, that is another story! Who knows?